Womanhood and Girlhood in Twenty-First Century Middle Class Kenya

Critical African Studies in Gender and Sexuality

Series Editors: Besi Brillian Muhonja (James Madison University) and Babacar M'Baye (Kent State University)

Advisory Board: Nkiru Nzegwu, Achola Pala, Melinda Adams, Binyavanga Wainaina, Ashley Currier, Betty Wambui, Jane Rarieya, Olufemi Taiwo, Cheikh Thiam

Critical African Studies in Gender and Sexuality publishes innovative, interdisciplinary research on intersections of gender, sexuality, and other political, social, economic, cultural, and geographic identity markers. The series has particular interest in groundbreaking scholarship on herstories/histories, elements and politics of gender and sexuality that center critical African thought and philosophies within global contemporary theoretical debates across the disciplines. Thus, manuscripts exploring gender relationships, queer identities, sexualities, masculinities, and femininities within both Africa and its Diaspora in interdisciplinary contexts are highly encouraged.

Womanhood and Girlhood in Twenty-First Century Middle Class Kenya: Disrupting Patri-centered Frameworks, by Besi Brillian Muhonja

Womanhood and Girlhood in Twenty-First Century Middle Class Kenya

Disrupting Patri-centered Frameworks

Besi Brillian Muhonja

LEXINGTON BOOKS
Lanham • Boulder • New York • London

Published by Lexington Books
An imprint of The Rowman & Littlefield Publishing Group, Inc.
4501 Forbes Boulevard, Suite 200, Lanham, Maryland 20706
www.rowman.com

Unit A, Whitacre Mews, 26-34 Stannary Street, London SE11 4AB

Copyright © 2018 by Lexington Books

All rights reserved. No part of this book may be reproduced in any form or by any electronic or mechanical means, including information storage and retrieval systems, without written permission from the publisher, except by a reviewer who may quote passages in a review.

British Library Cataloguing in Publication Information Available

Library of Congress Cataloging-in-Publication Data Available

ISBN 978-1-4985-3433-8 (cloth : alk. paper)
ISBN 978-1-4985-3434-5 (electronic)

∞™ The paper used in this publication meets the minimum requirements of American National Standard for Information Sciences Permanence of Paper for Printed Library Materials, ANSI/NISO Z39.48-1992.

For
Mama Hellen Muhonja Alumasa

Contents

Acknowledgments vii

Introduction: Middleclassness, Women, and Girls ix

1   Elective Lone Parenting, New Matrilines, and Matriarchies   1

2   *Usichana wa Ubabi*: Erasures of Ritual and the Myth of Independence   19

3   The Production of Bridehood   35

4   Wifing Bodies (Re)negotiating Selfhood   55

5   New Spaces, New Identities, New Languages   73

References 83

Index 97

About the Author 101

Acknowledgments

I find myself in the debt of many who have been a part of the process of making this book happen. I wish to first acknowledge the women and men who lent their voices and narratives to this work, which would not exist without their participation. I am not at liberty to share some of their names and the rest are too many to list. Asanteni sana. My gratitude goes to my family for inspiration, unwavering support, and unfailing love. I especially thank my mother, Hellen Muhonja Alumasa, and my sisters, Mideva, Kegehi, Kisia, and Buyanzi, who hold down the village while I disappear into my work, and who remain my biggest cheerleaders, and our children, Yvonne, Ivy, Shani, Adisa, Jeremy, Taye, and Eileen. It would be hard to do what I do without the constant presence and sustenance of my mentors Nkiru Nzegwu, Joanne Gabbin, David Owusu-Ansah, and Lamont King, and my brothers, Khadim Thiam and Evan Mwangi, and sister, Tammy Castle. To you I say, thank you for patience, love, and great insight through endless conversations and debates about this work, academia, and life.

I received support by way of debates, dialogue, comments, read-throughs, research suggestions, contacts, and design assistance from members of my extended academic and non-academic villages including Songi Lutomia, Achola Pala, Marame Gueye, Quito Swan, Mshai Mwangola, Mickie Mwanzia-Koster, Godwin Murunga, Betty Wambui, Wangui wa Goro, Peter Eubanks, Babacar M'Baye, Gillianne Obaso, Oyeronke Oyewumi, Shadrack Nasong'o, Muthoni Musangali, Tushabe wa Tushabe, Ndirangu wa Maina, Carolyn Imali, Brian Kiai, Peter Ng'ang'a, Ian Mbugua, Judy Kibinge, Flo Ndeda, Oyunga Pala, Ngele Ali, Abraham Ali, Felgonah Ndeda, Jameel Dennis, Terry Beitzel, Angela Rarieya, Irene Andia Mwema, Lilian Passos Wichert Feitosa, Austin Aluoch, Olufemi Taiwo, Ciru Miring'u, Francis Lutomia, Naijeria Toweett, Allan Aluvale, and Mercy Aluvale. Special thanks go to the founding members of the Project for African Decolonial and Indigenous Knowledges (PADIK), Tushabe wa Tushabe, Cheikh Thiam, Quito Swan, Mickie Mwanzia-Koster, Elias Bongmba, Bridget Awosika, and Tinu Maduagu, who offered great insights on segments of the book at a writing retreat in Nairobi, Kenya, in 2014. I am grateful to colleagues and friends who engaged the work of this book with me on conference panels and roundtables including Marame Gueye, Oyeronke Oyewumi, Tushabe wa Tushabe, Ian Foster, Peter Eubanks, Wairimu Njambi, Robert Goebel, Lamont King, and

Lilian Passos Wichert Feitosa. I am obligated to Consumer Insight for support with logistics and data access and Ndirangu wa Maina for offering a home in Nyeri, Kenya, to which I could retreat to write.

I thank my students at James Madison University, who made the exploration of this material in teaching a fulfilling experience, and my colleagues at JMU for the endless debates and sharing of our work, as well as collegiality, and general encouragement. Maureen Kegehi, Rony Wesonga, Barbara Monger, Rose Gray, Juan Mansilla, Morgan Paixao, and Carolyn Ware, thank you for helping manage the logistics of my plans for research and writing. I wish to thank Kevin Hegg, and the team at JMU Innovation Services for technological support during my research and writing, and my research assistants, Ivy Moraa, Faith Mueni, Gabrielle Henderson, Rebecca Klein, and October Edwards. I recognize the value of the financial support toward the production of this work from the following units at James Madison University: Provost's Summer Research Grant, Office of International Programs' International Development Grant, College of Arts and Letters Dean's International Travel Grant, the Office of Access and Inclusion, and College of Arts and Letters Educational Leave program.

Kate Tafelski, Emily Roderick, and the rest of the Lexington team, working with you has been an absolute pleasure.

Introduction

Middleclassness, Women, and Girls

Middle class Kenyan girl and women cultures are in common consideration, located, and, in so doing, often lost within the generalizing class-specific culture referred to as *ubabi*. *Ubabi* is a word in the Sheng slang language and was originally of the young anti-establishment self-proclaimed "ghetto population," but is now used across classes and ages. The word *ubabi* references attitudes, lifestyles, spaces, and cultures of the well-to-do. It is derived from the word "Babylon," translated as a place of plenty but also one that is easily corruptible. To members of the underclasses, it is the land of "the man," the privileged, the establishment. The very separation of *ubabi*, as middle-class and upper-class performances and ways of living is clear in the fact that the term was coined by the lower classes, to delineate their worlds and world senses from those of the middle class. *Ubabi*, thus, is inseparable from spending cultures as well as aspirational living and socializing. Kenyan girlhoods and womanhoods as a part of *ubabi* culture spawn their own highly influential distinct and unique subcultures, explored in this book in chapters traversing the identities of motherhood, coming-of-age girlhood, bridehood, and wifehood.

Twenty-first century girl and women cultures as statements on modern life must be understood as performances within specific cultural contexts. The contestation of the treatment of African women as a homogenous demographic erasing their multiformity has been a long-time exercise of scholars of critical African women's studies (Nzegwu, 1994, 1997, 2002, 2004, 2012; Mekgwe, 2008, 2010; Oyewumi, 1997, 2002; Pala, 1977, 2015). These and other scholars proffer approaches that can facilitate contextualized engagement with African female subjects. This book, a study of twenty-first century girlhoods and womanhoods, builds on this academic tradition. I legitimate the debates and arguments of this qualitative research production by concentrating on women and girls from a specific demographic with particular geographic, social, cultural, and economic markers. The book's interdisciplinary analysis and writing journeys through selected identities of girlhood and womanhood as ritualized by twenty-first century middle class Kenyans, and teases out the implications of these peculiarities to identity (re)creation and the restructuring of societies' structures, organs, and relationships.

The observations and arguments in the book are heavily supported by ethnographic and primary source research undertaken on the ground in the Nairobi, Nyeri, Kisumu, Mombasa, Machakos, Kakamega, Nakuru, Trans Nzoia, Uasin Ngishu, and Vihiga counties of Kenya.[1] Research carried out between May 2012 and February 2017 exposed a dearth of scholarly excursions into contemporary performances of girlhoods and womanhoods in Kenya. Outside of literary works and studies, majority of existing Africanist scholarship on Kenya into the conditions of girlhood, coming of age, bridehood, wifehood, and motherhood concentrate on pre-colonial and pre-independence indigenous communities and societies. This book, therefore, contributes to an area of scholarly urgency on Kenya. The chapters investigate questions related to a central point of inquiry: In a sex unequal, dynamic, multicultural cosmos, does operating under the jurisdiction of three cultural spaces with strong patriarchal underpinnings—religious, adopted foreign secular, and indigenous cultures—compound or assuage patriarchal influence on constructions and performances of girlhood and womanhood?

Paechter (2012) has cautioned against the juxtaposing of masculinities with femininities as others to each other, arguing that because such a set-up always begins with the masculine, this centers the hegemonic masculine in definitions of spaces and identities occupied by women, and in societies' structures and operations (p. 238). Other scholars go further, stressing the misplacement of such an approach particularly in engaging African subjects. Nzegwu (2004, 2012) underlines the limits of the metaphysics of gender, and Oyewumi (1997, 2002) decries feminism's continuous re-inventions of women that constantly regenerate focus on the masculine energy. In alignment with these thinkers, and applying a critical African studies lens, even though this is an examination into how female bodies and identities navigate their stake and agency under three patriarchal value systems, the arguments in this book center women as originators of action and thought without inquiring into a male other.

The choice to study womanhood and girlhood without deliberately juxtaposing these against masculine spaces and identities is itself a contestation of the gender binary framework. While in parts it is necessary to reference masculinity and maleness, these are not centered in the debates of the book's chapters. It is important to note here that the choice to study womanhood and girlhood is in no way intended as a statement on these as archetype female identities at the exclusion of others. Principally, this work is a disruption of patri-centered examinations into the conditions of girlhood and womanhood. The resulting deductions inform on the substratum of Kenyan girls and women's self-definitions, which are manifest in their experiences and ritualized practices, and articulate the impact of the performances of these bodies and identities on Kenyan and global societies.

Kenyan societies remain, in the twenty-first century, defined primarily as patrilineal and patriarchal (Wambui, 2013; Maseno and Kilonzo, 2011; Omwami, 2011; Rarieya, 2007; Odhiambo, 2007; Ligaga, 2012; Mutongi, 2007; Sanya, 2013). Patriarchally constructed girlhood and womanhood present in a chronology of customariness, and nonconformity to this order is often pigeonholed as deviant (Tamale, 2000; Ligaga, 2014; Sanya, 2013; Muhonja, 2015). Apposite patterns in the proper sequential order are, heterosexual filial daughter, dutiful wife, and virtuous and self-sacrificing mother. Bhabha (in Rutherford, 1990) imagines a third space—a location for contesting and re-drawing dominant narratives and practices, and such a deconstruction is discernible in new performances of womanhood and girlhood in Kenya. In what is an environment with transforming identity and role systems with new markers of success and cultural rectitude, how female members of society conceptualize efficacious womanhood is ever-changing. Because identities in cultural groupings are relational, these vicissitudes have bearings on the framing of society as a whole. It is this (re)framing that this work seeks to unpack.

This introduction offers a background against which the rest of the chapters may be understood, and particularizes the concepts and identities explored in the chapters that follow. This introduction, thus, examines the nature of Kenya's middle class, and delineates the terminology and concepts employed in the book including middleclassness, rituals, the different identities of womanhood and girlhood, and the three influencing cultures considered. I outline the colonial roots of a contemporary Kenyan middle class, whose character and rituals are embedded in three cultural worlds: indigenous, adopted foreign cultures, and religious. Although I recognize that some religious devotions and assemblies are foreign in origin, in this book I treat the two cultural spaces as distinct entities because they both have had momentous presence and influence on the creation of the space that is contemporary Kenya.

An elaboration on the three influencing cultural worlds considered in the book is necessary. First, are indigenous cultural practices and rituals, which colonialism as an integral part of the project of modernity sought to erase. Because the middle class during and following colonialism were imagined as the conveyers of "civilized" modern (read "European") living, which was married to the Christian religion, I also engage "westernization" and Christianity. As a carryover from colonial conceptualizations, "Westernized" is often a code word for progressive or civilized. I find this term problematic as I explain here. Westernization insinuates processes of becoming Western. But there exists no homogenous knowledge, culture, people, or political idea or space that one can refer to as Western, as applied in this sense. Additionally, using such a term contributes to discourses that equate progress with segments of the global North, but not even the entire global North, just Western Europe and North America. Unable to tie down what specific "West" is emulated in becoming Westernized, the concept of Westernization should be obliterated. In this book, I refer to European and American ways of being and cultures to denote the phenomenon traditionally labeled Westernization in Kenya. For the purposes of this book, European is used to represent only Western Europe, and American refers to the United States. I acknowledge the problematic of a reference to "European," that excludes Eastern Europe, and "American" that centers the United States at the exclusion of the rest of the Americas. This is necessitated by the fact that these are the two main foreign cultures influencing the Kenyan space, and American as an adjective and identity marker in common use often references the United States.

For most of the book I reference European and American cultures but, in sections of the book, I use the term Americanity. The state of cultural change present and always occurring in Kenya, I define, sometimes, as Americanity because while most Kenyans are quite equipped at elaborating on American lifestyles, language, politics, belief systems, and ways of being, the same cannot be said of their understanding or mastery of European and other global spaces. Often what is contemplated as "Westernization" in Kenya, and elsewhere, is Americanization (Owolabi, 2001; Mendis, 2005; Gakahu and Kaguta, 2011; Gray Shrestha and Nkansah, 2008). In relation to religion, Christianity is the reference point in this work because it is the most widely practiced faith in Kenya (Deacon and Lynch, 2015; McClendon and Riedl, 2015; Gez and Droz, 2015; Parsitau and Mwaura, 2010). Evangelicalism and neopentecostalism are the most common forms of Christianity practiced by Kenyans. The World Christian Database lists Kenya as having the fourteenth highest number of neopentecostal adherents in the world, making up 20 percent of Kenya's population (Deacon and Lynch, 2013, p. 230).

On the Kenyan space, it is easier to define blanket Christian and American/European cultures in a way that one cannot do with indigenous cultures. The challenge in defining monolithic or generalizing indigenous Kenyan cultural practices and entities emerges in scholarship because Kenyans belong to a variety of ethnic groups each with specific beliefs and traditions. I will, therefore, throughout this book draw from belief systems and traditions of various indigenous communities within Kenya to achieve credible, contextualized observations. That such an accommodation is necessary exemplifies the magnitude of this challenge. The very fact that Christianity and "Westernization" can each sell themselves as singular, powerful forces while ethnic group specific indigenous practices only impact segments of the population, suggests a heightening of the influence of these foreign entities on the creation and performances of present-day Kenyan womanhood and girlhood. Whatever the conclusions on this, one thing is clear: most Kenyans exist fluidly in a world where these three worlds intermingle and influence the lived experiences and rituals of women and girls.

This book interrogates performances of girlhoods and womanhoods in this multicultural world through a study of middle-class rituals and ways of being, and so, it is necessary to define the concept, ritual, as conceived by this work. Anthropologists and other scholars of culture have struggled with charting a conclusive definition of the concept "ritual" (Koster, 2011, p. 173). Leeds-Hurwitz (2002) defines rituals as being primarily about continuity (p. 89), and Rappaport (2002) extrapolates the features of ritual as "performance, formality, invariance, inclusion of both acts and utterances, encoding by other than the performers" (p. 24). I define rituals as recurrent tropes of individual and collective habitual practices that people invest time, financial, and other resources in, and that bear some form of stereotypy. Acquirement of practices and ceremonies that individuals choose to participate in with rigidity as an honored necessity ritualizes a behavior and its practice. Habitual practice institutionalizes and legitimizes rituals (Berado and Vera, 1981; Fiese, Tomcho, Douglas, Josephs, Poltrock, and Baker, 2002; Fiese, Hooker, Kotary, and Schwagler, 1993; Viere, 2001). Buy-in of the social human actors gives the rituals meaning and facilitates the construction of new identities or new representations of old identities. Public and private performances of the rituals articulate these new cultural and social identities, and enduring practice sustains and normalizes the new identities.

Rituals are born, transferred, and maintained under particular cultural sanctions, and understood structurally, functionally, and experientially. In the extreme, rituals create and sustain hegemonies, classifying, even gendering cultural practices and identities. Where different cultures converge, as is the case with the reality of middle class Kenyan women, locals sort through the different realities of culture flow and select traditions, which create a dynamic and new cultural universe. What constitutes the new culture manifests through the routine practice of the rituals they privilege? It is mostly from the three cultures defined above that Kenyans select the rituals that constitute "proper" performances of their womanhood and girlhood as well as their class status. In the following section, I expound on the class factor, specifically middleclassness and the Kenyan reality.

THE MIDDLE CLASS IN KENYA

The comprehensive definition of the concept of middleclassness and the identity ofKenyan middle class in this section of the introduction preempts the need for constant description of these two throughout the book. This strategy allows for a less distracted examination of girlhoods and womanhoods in the chapters that follow. The title of this book compels a number of questions. Does Kenya have a significant middle class, and if so, what characterizes it? Do Kenyan middle class rituals differ from those of other social groups? How do middle-class choices impact general societal constructions of identities? And what are the associations between class and the performance of identities, in this case, womanhood and girlhood?

Just like performing contemporary womanhood and girlhood, class stratification of Kenyan societies, and particularly the middle class, require more scholarly attention. Spronk (2014) observes that a number of the few studies available on this demographic in African studies have avoided directly referencing the social economic status (p. 97), explaining that while a small group of studies have used the term "middle class," the majority have preferred inquiry into the concept, "elite" (pp. 95–96). With the complexities attached to conceptualizing and deconstructing elitism, such studies would not speak exclusively or exhaustively about middle-class populations.

Most sociological research defines the middle class in terms of income and occupation, and consumption patterns, but there remains little consensus among scholars of different disciplines on what comprises the middle class. The query is further complicated by geographical, social, and political realities of the world's middle class (Ravallion, 2010; Banerjee and Duflo, 2008; Milanovic and Yitzhaki, 2002; Easterly, 2000; Birdsall, Graham, and Pettinato, 2000). Michael Ravallion (2010) explains that the measure of the developing world's middle class is often those not poor by standards of the developing world yet still poor by standards of countries such as the United States (p. 1). By this estimation, scholars characterize the middle class in the developing world as measured by belonging to a "household with consumption per capita between $2 and $13 a day at 2005 purchasing power parity" (Ravallion, 2010, p. 17). Per this definition, African Development Bank 2011 calculations placed Kenya's middle class at 6.48 million or 16.8 percent of the population, locating it as the fourth largest in sub-Saharan Africa (Ravallion, 2010, p. 1). Cheeseman (2014), who presents the middle class as fast expanding in Kenya (p. 649), deems such thresholds arbitrary. He highlights some problems with studies measuring the middle class based solely on consumption[2] (Cheeseman, 2014, p. 4), a position I support, and so, this commonly accepted definition of the developing world's middle class is not one I embrace in this book. I concur with the assertion of an expanding middle class, and underline Ravallion's (2010) statement that 1.2 billion new members of the middle class were created between 1990–2005 (p. 17) to highlight the middle class' capacity, by sheer numbers, to influence cultures.

Spronk (2014) aptly details that focusing on middleclassness offers insight into changes occurring culturally, economically, and socially across the African continent, and different forms of capital present in societies. She offers three factors that contribute to the condition of being middle class, which I borrow in this work. The scholar makes the case for a sociocultural based measure, considering, first, access to education and the type of occupations that result from that, primarily well salaried ones. Secondly, she cogitates on what I call economic, social, and cultural rituals manifest through consumption patterns and lifestyle choices. Modern self-perceptions wrap up the three factors. While the use of the term "modern" results in ambiguity, the point of self-identifying she makes is well taken. Resnick (2015), who imagines the state, entrepreneurship, and consumption as drivers of the middle class in sub-Saharan Africa, is in agreement with self-identification as a key marker. Like Spronk, Resnick (2015) highlights a crucial, and yet absent in scholarship, focus on "individuals' self-identification into this group and the presence of a middle class consciousness" (p. 10).

Spronk's definition of middleclassness as a practice very well complements my aspiration in this book to look at middle class being and doing. I focus on the satisfied middle class as well as the upper middle class in Kenya, what Homi Kharas in his paper, "The Emerging Middle Class in Developing Countries" (2010) refers to as the consumer class. Kharas captures the shifting designations of the developing world's middle class, and estimates middle-class numbers globally would be "the difference between the number of people with expenditures below the USD100 per day threshold and the number with expenditures below the USD10 per day threshold" (2010, p. 15). To a point, Kharas' classifications line up with the demographic Hatch, Becker, and Van Zyl (2011), in their estimation of five consumer segments in sub-Saharan Africa, refer to as cosmopolitan professionals and the upper level of rising strivers, and which Tschirley, Reardon, Dolislager, and Snyder (2015) denote as the non-vulnerable middle class.

In relation to Kenya's class stratification, Dieter and Stoll (2015) observe the presence of a "remarkable socio-cultural differentiation" (p. 3). They argue that comprehensively considering middle class' socioeconomic realities contests classical perceptions of class as socioculturally homogeneous. These observations hold true about Kenya's middle class. Because of its emergence in the age of globalization, the performance of a Kenyan middleclassness aspires more to the global standards than the "developing world" model defined by Ravallion. Kroeker, in theorizing Kenya's middle class, speaks of a blurring of the dichotomy between the global North and South (2014, p. 2). Kenya's middle-class adults can mostly cover basic family needs and enjoy some luxuries, some more than global North middle-class members. Indeed, because it is harder to access credit facilities in Kenya, people willing to invest or spend on luxury items and activities are often required to have disposable income more than their global North counterparts. Many members of the middle class have money leftover for leisure activities, savings, and investments, including property. This distinguishes the satisfied middle classers, and upper middle classers who are well salaried and/or wealth owners or creators, and who are the focus of this book, from the struggling middle class, which this book does not directly concentrate on.

Scholars have offered some economic, political, and cultural readings of Kenya's middle class. Murungi (2013) locates Kenya Vision 2030 as a middle class dream for Kenya as a place with "modern infrastructure, cosmopolitan consumers, professional workers, and international connections" (p. 21). With this creation of a neo-liberal space, Manji (2015) argues, in relation to Nairobi's infrastructural development, that the less affluent are experiencing marginalization as they are priced out of living spaces and this is redefining the idea of "right to Nairobi" (p. 219). This thinking underscores the separation of the Kenyan middle-class space from others, and the cultural, social, and political impact of the middle class. Of Kenya's middle class, Cheeseman (2014) presents, aligning with Spronk's argument for access to education as a defining factor, that they are well educated locally and/or abroad, are technologically hooked-in, and enjoy networks not limited to the Kenyan space. He offers them as politically engaged, even though some have accused the Kenyan middle class of being too complacent politically.

While expanding the definition beyond consumption, it is important to note that Kenya's middle-class culture is highly consumerist, and class members like to visibly sport markers of their success (Spronk, 2014; Murungi, 2013). They like to be identified as residing in middle class neighborhoods, which are often comfortable with easy access to necessary conveniences and luxury services. These homes range from the very expensive to what are considered middle-income neighborhoods. It is, however, impossible to lock down which class members have more money based on location of residence. In the capital city, Nairobi, for example, many middle-class members who own their homes and make a good living have residences in South B, Embakasi, South C, Buruburu, Lang'ata, Nairobi West, along Mombasa Road all the way to the Athi River, and other similar neighborhoods. On the other hand, there are middle-class members who do not own their homes and have little by way of savings, but rent and live in what might be considered more upscale neighborhoods like Kilimani, Loresho, Lavington, Westlands, Gigiri, and Riverside. Ndirangu wa Maina, group managing director of Consumer Insight, a leading market research company operating across Africa, underscores the significance of considering net worth in computations of social class (personal communication, February 13, 2017). While not all Kenyan middle classers attain all of the items listed here, middle-class aspirations in Kenya include owning a home and/or other property, car ownership, affording private school and providing college education for their children, retiring comfortably, having the capacity to afford insurance for family health and property, and having disposable income for recreation and leisure. It is in the pursuit of these dreams that some find themselves perpetually in the comfortable middle class but with a net worth that does not increase, or stuck in the struggling middle class.

The foregoing clarification about the different strata of Kenyan middle-class members leads to a notation that there is a group that performs middleclassness differently, particularly in Kenya's urban centers. They choose to not live in the expensive neighborhoods, and some build or buy homes on the outskirts of the cities where they work, for example around Nairobi, in Ngong, Ongata Rongai, Kitengela, Ruai, Rimpa, and Mlolongo, among others. This group may send their children to more affordable schools and cut back on luxury spending in order to direct funds in investments and for building wealth and future expenditures. In many other ways, though, they enjoy the visible trappings of middle-class existence and habits of the rest of Kenyan middle classers.

Another group of middle classers that are recognized through considering Spronk and Resnick's (2015) tendering of self-definition as a marker of middleclassness exists. This demographic are identifiable primarily through their own claims to being middle class. This is the group of Kenyans who attempt to live as the comfortable middle class do, but fall in the lower middle-class category by the standards defined in this book. Still, their cultures and those of the less struggling and more satisfied middle class among Kenyans are sometimes the same precisely because those in the lower middle class aspire to be, and so, self-define and attempt to live like the thriving middle class. Thus, while they may not have the capacity to afford some of the prescriptive middle-class traditions and accouterments, they aspire to them, and in fact try to live up to middle-class standards, or adapt the habits to their standards. For example, in Nairobi, to attain the middle-class appearance by wearing designer clothes, they go to or have shoppers go on their behalf to Toi, Gikomba, or other secondhand items markets where they can purchase used clothes shipped into the country. According to Mutahi, a personal shopper with over twenty clients, prices for these clothes and accessories, which have traditionally been very low, are in fact being driven up dramatically by middle class members' patronizing of these markets[3] (Mutahi, personal communication, February 7, 2017). Because of this character of the lower middle class, the arguments in this book, while mostly studying the ways of the satisfied middle class and upper middle class, could be extrapolated to apply to the lower middle class as well. In fact, their inclusion in calculating numbers of those practicing middle-class rituals allows for an appreciation of the augmented cultural and social influence of middle class Kenyans. While collecting research for this book, I noted that many lower middle-class members are heavily invested doing middleclassness. As one interviewee states, "We fake it till we make it. Our children need to know they can make it in this life too" (Agufwa, personal communication, May 29, 2014).

Spronk reminds us that "a consideration of class as an aspirational category and the ways in which it is practiced allows us to see that forms of capital that are not, strictly speaking, economic, are central to understanding middle-class formation" (p. 111). Entry into the middle class remains the first marker of significant economic success in Kenyan societies, and it is the first economic class that most Kenyan's proudly claim belonging to and flaunt. Many Kenyan's post-independence started off from a location of marginalization, and so the desire to be middle class, to rise up the ladder, became a common goal. The need and choice to belong was, and remains deliberate, even urgent. Rituals of the middle class, therefore, set the standards of cultural, economic, and social life. Middle-class members, because of their economic, social, and political location and agency, affirm social trends, and almost always spearhead the borrowing of outside influences and standards of social practice, making them an important demographic through which to explore the (re)creation of identities in a globalized reality.

By comparison, upper-class members of society in Kenya are very few in number, minimizing their impact. As Hatch et al. (2011) note, "The affluent of Africa have disproportionately high purchasing power, and are considered wealthy regardless of where they travel across the globe. This group is extremely small and very fickle" (p. 18). They are also more attached to practices, some very old, that define them as different from everyone else and so they bow to external influence more cautiously. Upper-class members typically "play" in private within very exclusive circles, and often on global platforms. Their impact in passing on or even the desire to share cultural rituals is therefore not as present as it is with the middle class. Additionally, most citizens consider the middle class attainable. The wealthy upper class, on the other hand, remain out of reach for most, and so the struggling classes do not invest in working toward it. Because few achieve upper-class status, the middle class is the epitome of success and thus the aspirational goal for many. This is part of what drives the desire to perform middle-class rituals as soon as one is able to, sometimes before one can comfortably afford them.

For the reasons outlined above, middle-class preferences in terms of cultural rituals impact the hierarchical organization of societal practices, and this informs particular ways of performing middleclassness. Processes of coding middle-class living involve the creation of ideal social institutions for and by the middle class. Thus, as soon as one is able to claim affinity to the middle class, their ways of being and rituals change significantly. Middle classers, in this way, regulate cultural transferences in society, including, for women and girls. In the following section, I historicize the birth of these ways of being and performing contemporary Kenyan middle-class culture. This will be invaluable in appreciating the arguments on assimilation, conformity, and traditionalism in the book, and the effects of the convergence of European/American, Christian, and indigenous cultural influences on performances of girlhoods and womanhoods.

The Colonial Heritages of Kenya's "Modern" Middle Class

Studies across the disciplines on Kenya's contemporary middle class remain scarce precisely because as a result of colonial interruption, it is still in its emergent years, and still in the process of fashioning itself. While some studies indicate a birth of the social group earlier, specifically during the colonial era (Sklar, 1963; Rana, 1977; Cowen, 1976), they engage the idea of the middle class at a time when a modern African middle class, as defined for the purposes of this book, was very small. Regarded through the colonial lens and societal structuring, Africans were framed as lacking capacity to access the upper classes. It is the very small group of African Kenyan middle classers established in colonial Kenya that informed studies on the formation of the middle class that Resnick (2015) expounds on, teasing out the influence of Marxist ideology and traditions in the radical 1960s on this scholarship. The birth of a robust contemporary middle class in Kenya, as in most colonized and developing nations, is a post-independence phenomenon.

The colonial construction of modern Kenya's middle class was accompanied by religious persuasions. Today's middle class in Kenya was born out of the colonial and Christian organizing of bodies. Both Christianity and colonialism invested in projects to rewrite identities. This was necessary for the creation of a hierarchy of not just bodies politically, socially, and economically, but also of cultures, a mainstay of colonialism. Alongside the colonial investment in a creation of a racially defined middle and upper class "us" distinct from a lower class, clearly marked for "them," the Africans, was the Christian definition of proper living differentiated from deviance. To ensure success of this mission that demonized African cultures and practices as uncivilized and deviant, limited access to middle-class environments was extended to the "educated" and "civilized" Christian Africans that would join the ranks of the middle class as providers of services primarily for the Europeans, or to assist in the project of ruling the "natives" while the rest of the Africans remained an aberration to the colonial establishment (Muhonja, 2014; Kanogo, 2005; Shaw, 1995; Christopher, 1988).

This configuration of bodies meant that the rewriting of identities was accompanied by upward mobility and better treatment for some Africans. Here began the training of the populace to desire modern middleclassness, and the aspirational element of middleclassness. This also was part of the activation of modern designing of the appropriate location of good and bad female bodies. It is out of this history that "ladies," as defined by European and American cultures, were born in Kenya. Until then, many Kenyan communities did not, in fact, have an equivalent term to "lady." Gendered definitions of respectability determined expectations of proper behavior for "educated," "religious," and "civilized" ladies (Kanogo, 1993; Muhonja, 2010; Gaidzanwa, 2003; Thomas, 2000). This formulation of the middle class was inherited and carried forward lock, stock, and barrel into post-independence Kenya. The mannerisms, inclusions, and exclusions of the middle class were heartily embraced by the new Kenyan haves, and denied to the have-nots. Comprehending this movement and (re)location of bodies allows for an awareness of the exclusionary nature, as well as the patriarchal personality of middle-class Kenyan societies today as maintained by the same cultural influences that created this middle class itself during colonialism. In the paragraphs that follow, I appraise the cultural adjustments that transpire at the meeting of three cultural influences.

Adaptation and performance of contemporary middle-class Kenyan women's and girls' rituals demonstrate culture flows and intercourses that occur with the interactions of different worlds. Proliferation of easily accessible and disseminated technology and media heightens the swiftness with which cultural practices are dispersed or relocated, (re)created, adapted, and adopted within middle-class spaces globally. Capacity to reach large numbers of people at the same time, and for those people to easily share experiences promotes processes of mass introduction to new concepts and ideas. In Kenya, this initiates and then wears down the tensions and contradictions of rituals from different cultural influences, attempting a form of cultural homogenization (Nyamnjoh, 2011; Ndlela, 2009).

The interfacing of two or more major cultures induces the process of acculturation. Acculturation itself prompts changes to all active cultures, and for individuals, this is accompanied by psychological and physical adjustments. The multiculturalism that exemplifies middle-class Kenyan culture is easy to demonstrate. What remains untracked is the bi- or cross-directionality of that acculturation, and how much the different interacting cultures influence each other to affect the construction of modern day Kenyan womanhood and girlhood. This is a primary interest of this book. It is hard to lock down the processes of enculturation and acculturation in studying the middle-class populations of Kenya. The challenge, in some ways, a consequence of colonialism, lies in identifying what to define as the first culture that would help one understand the process of absorbing the second or third culture. What, in fact, are middle-class Kenyan girls' first cultures when they know next to nothing about their indigenous cultures that would have, perhaps, grounded their identity? A few other circumstances also complicate such a process. How does one process a situation where the first culture of a family or a group was specifically lower class related but they now enjoy a middle-class existence? How does one manage situations where the first culture has since been completely shed and discounted? What if parents were raised with indigenous cultural values but the children lack any cultural or social rootedness in that system? What if parents grew up lower class and the children have been born and raised middle class? This is the dilemma one encounters in trying to define processes of culture change and mixing for Kenyan middle-class women and girls.

The desire for social mobility that characterizes middle-class living and being leaves its members susceptible to the persuasions of cultural assimilation, often without alertness to where or how their original indigenous culture is represented or affected. Accordingly, for Kenya's middle-class female members, particularly the young, the most significant influencing cultures *appear* to be European/American, and religious. Spronk observes about young middle class Kenyans in Nairobi that their social networks, churches, and neighborhoods are interethnic (p. 104). Using the narrative of a middle-class couple's wedding, she illustrates how the young cope with this dilemma. The scholar explains that tensions were present between their two families, which were from different ethnic groups, and to manage the crisis, the couple designed the wedding to showcase a lack of favoring of either culture. The second part of her observation highlights not just the multicultural nature of many middle class spaces and events, but also allows us to deduce the erasure of certain indigenous particularities, and reflect on what replaces them.

The tensions of cultural glocalization coupled with the colonial legacy that presents a hierarchy of cultures, provokes a partial or total erasure of certain traditions, enhancement of others, and the ultimate creation of new ever-metamorphosing middle-class cultures, girlhoods, and womanhoods. Even though, with the passing of time, some cultures appear to overwhelm others; this demographic is engaged in a constant harmonizing of cross-cultural rituals. In this environment, the female Kenyan body performing new multicultural rituals—navigating, erasing, and adopting—is an identity that offers new understandings of contestations and conformity in relation to patriarchal expectations. These bodies are sites for (re)creation, because whether operating in resistance or acquiescence, what they birth are complex identities representing different spiritual, social, and cultural dimensions of girlhood and womanhood. These emerging bodies and identities are the focus of the chapters that follow.

Girls and Women of Kenya's Twenty-First Century Middle Class

The chapters in this book are organized to privilege the mother's relationship to progeny (Oyewumi, 2002, p. 5), and divorce motherhood from wifehood. They journey through the identities motherhood, coming-of-age girlhood, bridehood, and wifehood, in that order. The sacred nature of the mother identity, as central to the processes of creation of human life, bestows on women honor and power within the physical and spiritual realms in all indigenous Kenyan communities' world-senses

(Kabaji, 2009; Mbiti, 1990; Pala, 2015). I explore, in chapter 1, the question of whether contemporary Kenyan motherhood, especially among Kenya's middle class, maintains this veneration. There are, admittedly, complexities attached to measuring a non-set value, and so, endeavors to respond to the question unsheathe auxiliary inquiries. These include whether or not middle-class women prioritize motherhood, and what the value of motherhood is in this fast evolving demographic with new and varied measures for success.

Changing dynamics in relation to what, when, why, for whom, and how motherhood fits into women's lives, and the systematic erasure of collective living in middle class Kenya are some factors reorganizing the players and rituals of mothering and motherwork. In this world, motherhood's encounters with performances of diverse modern-day personhoods and identities of Kenyan women inform the crafting of new family alternatives and maternal identities. A broader range of family models with new constructions of motherhood, along with new technologies and tools of modern living affect the daily routines and rituals of women and mothers, and women as mothers. Choices of women to mother or not, and to mother as wives or not, confront long held conceptions rooted in patriarchy, and patriliny about these identities.

Transformations in motherhood and mothering processes are a part of a larger upheaval occurring in parenting cultures in Kenya. Like mothers, girls, too, find themselves steering through an ever-changing terrain of relationships in culturally hybridized environments. Where once parents invested heavily in coming-of-age processes, indications from the research for this book are that such processes and conversation have been watered down among the middle class. For various reasons, including those explored in chapter 2, the deficiency of dialogue on the coming-of-age process in academic research on Kenya is replicated in real-life family practices. In scholarship, coming-of-age narratives have been abridged to readings of female genital cutting, child bridehood, and explorations of sexual and reproductive health. In Kenya's middle-class families, there is a glaring absence of processes of initiation into culture-specific adult ways of knowing and being. It is important to note that initiation, here, as explained in chapter 2, does not refer to genital modifications.

The erasure of processes of initiation, along with the collapsing of the identities and roles of alloparents and other mothers into the ubiquitous "Auntie," induce new ways to symbolize, celebrate, and structure the world of girls coming-of-age. In reality, rituals of coming-of-age have been reduced to shopping for the first bra, first pair of high heeled shoes, introduction to makeup, and the establishment of first social media pages, with little in depth accompanying impartation of skills and knowledge toward maturity. Kanini, the mother of a teenage girl argues in defense of parents that, "Sometimes I feel like she is parenting me. They know so much more than we knew, so much sooner than we did" (personal communication, January 9, 2017).

With a lack of proper societal systems to assist, for many, what is supposed to be a long process is reduced to one event commonly referred to as "the talk." Such a subversion of practices of socializing girls has repercussions for how they transition into womanhood. The lack of arbitrated rootedness in a coming-of-age institution suggests a process free of adult supervision and cultural adjudication. The resulting unfixed experience of the coming-of-age process infers a liberated coming-of-age girlhood, and compels interesting considerations for questions of maturity, autonomy and agency for girls, explored in chapter 2.

Like motherhood and girlhood, contemporary bridehood and weddings, studied in chapter 3, have received almost no attention in scholarship on Kenya. The significance of bridehood and weddings as sites for studying performances of classed identities is, by implication, captured in Julia Pauli's study of weddings in Fransfontein, Namibia. She observes that "weddings have become the most important arena for expressing class distinction. In no other area of life has the emerging elite of politicians and professionals invested as much money and creativity to exhibit and celebrate their distinctiveness as they do in weddings" (Pauli, 2013, p. 154). Spronk paints a vivid picture of this exhibitionist character of weddings in the description of a wedding of a young middle-class Nairobi couple: "For their wedding they rented a lush garden and put up white tents adorned with white ribbons. There was an enormous wedding cake, a band, and hundreds of visitors" (p. 102).

Weddings are rituals, which facilitate the bridal body's transition into a wifing body. "Bride" as metonym is commonly used to reference a woman who is about to get married or a newly wed woman. What is lacking is clarity on when bridehood ends and wifehood begins. Traditionally, regardless of the statement, "I now pronounce you husband and wife," in the first year of marriage many cultures use the terms wife and bride interchangeably. In a contrast that is reductionist to womanhood in comparison to manhood, no state of groomhood exists beyond the wedding rituals. Upon declaration of a marriage, the man transforms magically into a husband, requiring no transitioning period or testing. The following statement, used at most weddings, is telling: "I now declare you husband and wife. You may kiss your bride!" Readings of practices of the Luhya, Gikuyu, and Luo, as representative of other indigenous communities of Kenya, allow for the inference that they marked the end of bridehood with the birth of a child. Consider the fact that a married woman, in all three cultures, was not allowed full access to activities in their new home, including cooking in some communities like the Maragoli, until she had birthed a child. In this imaginary, a bride, therefore, would transition into complete wifehood with motherhood. Per this conceptualization, the first year of marriage is a period of transition from bridehood to wifehood. Proper brideliness, while learning the rituals of wifehood, determines a bride's successful installation into her new family.

A close examination of rituals determines a parallel to this conception in Christian and secular European/American practices. Middle class Kenyans save the top tier of the wedding cake, which they consume on the first anniversary of their wedding. The roots of this ritual are quite revealing. It is borrowed from an English practice, where until the nineteenth century the cakes in question were easy to preserve liqueur-soaked fruitcakes. They would use this to celebrate the christening of the first child (Roney et al., 2014; A little Cake Place). The timing of the christening ceremony when combined with the consumption of the cake at the first year anniversary is informative. It mimics the secular definition of bridehood as ending with the first year of marriage because the christening suggests that the bride is expected to have become pregnant and had a child. The Bible verse Deuteronomy 24:5 (New King James Version) supports the assessment that the first year is viewed even by cultures that birthed Christianity as a year of transition. It reads, "When a man has taken a new wife, he shall not go out to war or be charged with any business; he shall be free at home one year, and bring happiness to his wife whom he has taken." Such happiness, if one considers layered meanings of the statement "bring happiness to his wife," and the christening ceremony of English practice, would hopefully climax in childbirth.

Across Christian, indigenous Kenyan, and secular European and American cultures, there seems to be a meeting of thoughts marrying bridehood and wifehood to motherhood. Indigenous Kenyan cultures enjoy a broader definition of motherhood, which delimits its absolute marriage to wifehood (Pala, 2013). Still, in indigenous Kenyan communities, most of them patriarchal, bio-motherhood was expected to arrive via wifehood. In all these cultures, the expectations on the bridal body are clear, and exemplify societies' need to keep female bodies under control. Expected of the bride is safeguarded virginity until marriage followed by immediate birthing of children. This speedy changeover into motherhood allowed societies a quick assessment of the fecundity of the bride within the first year before considering her a worthy wife. As such, bridehood is traditionally envisioned as a temporary state where one's value or worth as a wife is tested. For the purposes of this book, I conceive middle-class Kenyan bridehood, and all bridehoods, like groomhood, as shed the moment the declaration of marriage is made.

Kenya's twenty-first century middle-class bridal practices present as what Leeds-Hurwitz (2002), citing Levi-Strauss (1966), refers to as a bricolage, the "bringing together of previously used signs into new (and unexpected) combinations [. . . and a] cultural recycling" (p. 87). Rituals almost always have some cultural, political, spiritual, or social value, but that value is not always quantifiable. Leeds-Hurwitz's typifies a symbol as a kind of sign where the correlation between the visible and implicit qualities is arbitrary. Although rituals tend to be scripted, rigid, repetitive, and holding collective value, they are not always symbolic (Rappaport, 2002), and sometimes, their value is situated in nothing more than personal gratification. Among Kenyan brides, human anxiety attached to the need to belong as part of the middle class has motivated widespread participation in, and facilitated the easy spread of European and American bridal practices. Most Christian middle-class Kenyan brides from all ethnic backgrounds partake in European, American, and Christian originated rituals, and only those from within specific indigenous communities practice their rituals. The question that emerges is whether, in the construction of a contemporary middle-class bridehood, Christianity and secular foreign models provide the primary blueprints, and so have the greatest influence on constructions of bridal and, consequently, wifing identities.

The desire to be a wife or not, rituals of selecting mates, and how women interested in marriage conceptualize wifehood, contribute to the creation of a Kenyan middle-class bridal identity. The modern middle-class bride is generally prepped for wifehood within a nuclear family model with roles defined through colonial era and Christian gendering interventions (Kanogo, 2005). These have historically contributed heavily to the process of making vulnerable the wifing female body. Good wifehood in contemporary Kenya responds to expectations of the three heavily moralizing patriarchal cultures deliberated in this book. The anatomy of a good wife submitted at church weddings is presented as chaste, compliant, friendly, productive, and servant to family (Proverbs 31),[4] and endorsed by various biblical narratives.[5] How present day middle-class wifing bodies in Kenya navigate patriarchal pressures, roles, duties, and relations is engendering new womanhoods within marriages, and new masculinities and femininities. As a result, like motherhood, bridehood, and coming-of-age, middle-class performances of wifehood are restructuring families and societies. I explore the future developments as well as implications of these performances in the final chapter of the book.

In contemporary Kenyan societies and institutions, contradictions inherent even within one of the three patriarchal cultures this book engages complicate any attempts at simple definitions of Kenyan womanhoods or girlhoods. The secular deinstitutionalization of marriage, restructuring of families, Africanization of Christianity, secularization of Christian values and the birth of charismatic churches, and adjustments to definitions of what is conservative or liberal demand new critical approaches and tools for characterizing and studying women and girls. In this book, I attempt such a critical analysis of performances of womanhoods and girlhoods using frameworks and lenses that center the female players.

CONCLUSION

Twenty-first century Kenya, fashioned through processes of globalization and the formation of the nation-state, is a site where local worlds and senses interrelate with global entities and domains. The resulting cultural mosaics demand inquiries into what to privilege in defining a middle-class culture. One sure way to determine this is through observing rituals of the class members. How middle class Kenyans navigate different dimensions of cultural globalization spawns new social and cultural entities, and transmutes identities and personhoods dispensing new girlhoods and womanhoods. New rituals of girlhood and womanhood that materialize when religious, indigenous, and foreign worlds encounter each other are re-structuring family and society, and recasting roles. This examination of Kenya's middle class allows for an appreciation of how contemporary social performances of femaleness are disrupting and complicating conceptions of gender and gendered spaces. This must in turn transform and alter scholarship and create new responsive plots on and for African girls and women.

NOTES

1. Most of the participants in the research for this work are based in Nairobi. This being the first time, for all of them, participating in a study like this, a significant number requested a change of their names to protect their privacy.

2. "Another major problem with measuring the middle class solely in terms of consumption is that some of the classic analyses of class had as much to say about employment status and education as they did about income and expenditure" (Cheeseman, 2014, p. 4).

3. Not only members of the lower middle class shop at these markets or use shoppers. Satisfied middle-class members also patronize these businesses.

4. Five evangelical pastors reveal that besides Proverbs 31, there exists a set of ubiquitous bible readings used at most Christian wedding ceremonies or marriage counseling sessions. Rarely does one select readings outside of this set, which includes 1 Corinthians 13:4–13; Matthew 19:4–6; 1 John 4:16–19; Song of Solomon 8:6; Genesis 2:18–24; Ruth 1:16–17; Ephesians 5:22–33; Proverbs 18:21; Ecclesiastes 4:9-12; Philippians 4:4–9; Colossians 3:12–19.

5. 1 Corinthians 13:4–13; Matthew 19:4–6; 1 John 4:16–19; Song of Solomon 8:6; Genesis 2:18–24; Ruth 1:16–17; Ephesians 5:22–33; Proverbs 18:21; Ecclesiastes 4:9–12; Philippians 4:4–9; Colossians 3:12–19. The church also counsels in accordance with 2 Corinthians 6:14: "Be ye not unequally yoked together with unbelievers: for what fellowship hath righteousness with unrighteousness? And what communion hath light with darkness?"

ONE
Elective Lone Parenting, New Matrilines, and Matriarchies

This qualitative study contests the moralizing of select personhoods that equates married motherhood to fulfilled womanhood by examining a growing yet rarely addressed group of women in Kenya—partner free professional women in their late thirties to early fifties. Their experiences are instructing new constructions of womanhood, which are generating novel motherhoods and matriarchies. Choices of alternative approaches to attaining motherhood by this, until now, uninvestigated set of individuals, are rewriting conceptions of womanhood, and with it, family, as well as the concepts matriarchy and patriarchy. Rituals and demands of professional womanhood, which define a single professional woman's (SPW) social and career patterns, sometimes lead to single adulthood and/or delayed parenthood. Increasingly, for a plethora of reasons, more SPWs in urban Kenya are not participating in rituals of bridehood and wifehood. This demographic is augmented by numbers of divorced SPWs. This, in many ways, actuates women's states and performances of identities that can result in contestations of patriarchal womanhood and motherhood, which are limited by the fact that they are defined in relation to men.

This inquiry into maternal rituals, cultures, and processes, designates and delineates what I christen elective lone parenthood (ELP) as distinct from single motherhood. Oyewumi (2002) points out the oxymoronic character of the moniker "single mother" stating, "From an African perspective and as a matter of fact, mothers by definition cannot be single. In most cultures, motherhood is defined as a relationship to progeny, not as a sexual relationship to a man" (p. 5). This observation is affirmed by indigenous African conceptualizations of motherhood (Pala, 2013; Nzegwu, 2004), as well as by phenomena in contemporary Kenya that are calling attention to the complexity of motherhood. These include increased diversity in family forms and the emergence of new avenues to bio-motherhood. Focusing on bio-motherhood and other legally recognized motherhoods, I examine motherhood as influenced by contemporary technological, cultural, economic, and social nonconformities in a space where properties of indigenous, religious, and European/American cultures encounter each other.

Maternal spaces complementary to bio-motherhood, including assisted reproductive technologies such as surrogacy or gestational carriers, and in vitro fertilization (IVF), as well as processes of accessing nonbiological parenthood through adoption, demand fresh rituals toward creating and legitimating family status. Of the ever-rising numbers of what I call partner-free or SPWs in urban Kenya, a segment are opting to pursue motherhood and mothering without a parenting partner who is a significant other, participating in what I categorize as elective lone parenting (ELP). Narratives of ELPs provide insight into how changes in scheduling, patterns, and presentation of maternity are repositioning motherhood in relation to fatherhood, and womanhood in relation to manhood. The analysis here further highlights reconfigurations in motherhood's association with the identities woman and wife in ways that are transforming notions of proper and acceptable adult womanhood per patriarchal characterization.

To render a picture truly reflective of the number of women willing to partake in ELP, I lead with an expose of the levels of participation and interest. To make this determination, I consider available figures from assisted reproductive technologies (ART) specialists as well as challenges discouraging participation by many willing women. I then interrogate the capacity of ELP, as differentiated from other forms of lone parenting, as efficient cause to modifications in societies' organizing principles and language, to allow for an appreciation of the vast epistemic and social implications of this phenomenon. I conclude by outlining the impact of ELP on patriliny and patriarchy, gendered familial identities, and the foundation of new matriarchies and matrilines to ultimately distinguish a maturation of new womanhoods.

In order to comprehend the implications, by numbers, of this trend, it is important to recognize that the challenges and anxieties outlined within the chapter overwhelm the great desire to explore ELP for many women. Different motivations curb SPW's pursuit of ART delivered bio-motherhood, surrogacy, or adoption as ELPs. For example, with adoption, the investment required in creating for the adoptee assurance of belonging, the creation and validation of a dual heritage, and management of healing from trauma and other emotional needs can be particularly daunting for a busy lone parent. Still, the numbers of those participating in ELP continue to rise, and as circumstances change legally and there's a diminution of stigma, the numbers will, undoubtedly, increase exponentially.

Of the thirty-two SPWs who participated in this qualitative research between May 2013 and January 2017, twelve were committed to ELP, thirteen said they would if they had the resources and support, while the remaining were dissuaded by their religious beliefs and uncertainty related to fear of taking the journey alone. The significance, according to Dr. Patel[1] who says the movement cannot be reversed, is in the growing numbers of women willing to consider ELP even amid obvious challenges. At Dr. Patel's clinic, as of July 2014, of every one hundred ART clients who went through with the procedures, about six were single women. The number of single women consulting on various procedures was much higher, sometimes as much as 200 percent more (personal communication, July 24, 2014). These elevated figures of willing players are an indicator for projections on the numbers of ELP families in the future. An examination of the reasons holding women back follows, and can inform such forecasting.

During this research I encountered women who, content or not, accept their status and settle into a childless existence, mostly persuaded by religiosity. Christianity propositions double-edged influence. In performing Christian womanhood, absent parenthood is often attributed to God's purpose. However, this determination does not always match the women's yearning because they view motherhood as part of God's plan for women. They rationalize that they trust God's will and yet, for those interested in motherhood, this trust appears to not assuage their disappointment at being denied motherhood. Religious and other stigma attached to not getting married means that women planning to have children alone are still the subjects of incredulity. This stigma is rooted, in part, in the society's belief in the nuclear family and conjugal partner co-parenting. Questions and statements of disapproval directed at SPWs considering ELP overlook the fact that for a variety of reasons, including divorce, there are already many Kenyan mothers parenting "singly."

Dr. Patel and Dr. Noreh,[2] leading ART specialists in the country, explain that societal disapproval is not the only deterrent for SPWs interested in ELP. They clarify that the available facilities in Kenya are state of the art and yet anxieties about the newness of some assisted reproductive technology services in Kenya persist. Further, hurdles of sperm acquisition, to be elaborated on at a later point in the chapter, and steep procedural expenses discourage many women from participating. Concerns about expenses are not mitigated by the fact that no local medical insurance company covers assisted reproductive technology procedures in Kenya and women are forced to source this internationally at great expense (personal communications, July, 2014). It is indeed fathomable that insurance companies are afraid of the avalanche of women who would sign up for these procedures if coverage were to become available locally. Fear occasioned by the knowledge that the majority of women who undergo ART procedures at an older age do not succeed is another deterrent according to the specialists and the women in this study. The most popular procedure at Dr. Patel's clinic and at the Nairobi IVF Center is intracytoplasmic sperm injection (ICSI), however, it has a 60 percent failure rate. This is further complicated by the fact that most SPWs considering ART are in their late thirties to mid-forties, a demographic with an even higher failure rate.

The challenges summarized above compel alternative routes to bio-motherhood, specifically the use of surrogate mothers and gestational carriers. The question of parental rights muddles surrogacy in Kenya, discouraging even more women from participating in ART processes. At birth, the laws of Kenya recognize only the birth mother, in this case, the surrogate mother, forcing women who use surrogates to have to adopt their own children increasing the emotional and financial burden.[3] Between healthcare, gynecology fees, legal fees for adoption processes, living expenses, and surrogate fees, the cost for a surrogacy process, by August 2014 estimates, came to about two million Kenya shillings.[4] And always present is the fear of being held at ransom by the surrogate mother who could change her mind.

These hindrances to participation are at once a curse and a blessing for the system. By 2014, there were only six IVF centers in Kenya, a fact that restricts access and raises costs as monopolies tend to do. Access to services is limited and the systems are overwhelmed. For some busy or fearful SPWs, the impediments offer justifications for surrendering their strong desire to be ELPs. They submit as reasons: lack of time off work to deal with hormonal treatments, possible side effects, and post-natal childcare commitments for career women in single income homes for whom, in fact, the jobs are essential to pay for the procedures, and the child afterwards. Potential ELPs are also apprehensive about the penalty of motherhood (England et al, 2016; Kahn et al, 2014; Gash, 2009; Anderson et al, 2003), which can be especially brutal for women parenting alone.[5] Exacerbating this is a financial burden that many of the women bear as a function of the absence of direct motherhood. Because they do not have children, there are assumptions from their extended families that SPWs have disposable finances. Nduta's[6] statement captures this aptly: "People, and by that I mean my family, think that just because I don't have children, I have money that has no work. It just sits there, they think. So where am I getting money to pursue motherhood?" (personal communication, July 25, 2014). This financial dilemma would be easier to address if the ELPs could unreservedly communicate their plans to family and friends. Yet ELPs and potential ELPs prefer to keep their plans private to avoid courting castigation and judgment, and also to self-protect emotionally in the event that ART fails them. As a consequence, they find themselves on very lonely journeys. The idea of bearing that loneliness accompanied by a number of other subjective reservations that trigger understandable reactions from women who express an interest in mothering alone is enough to discourage many.

What is clear from conversations with medical specialists, SPWs, ELPs and potential ELPs is that with fewer challenges and increased tolerance, the number of women freely engaging in ELP will undoubtedly rise. According to Dr. Patel, leading specialists in the ART field in Kenya have created a consortium to lobby for certain developments including recognition of rights of parents using surrogates and insurance for ART procedures. Additionally, the group seeks to institute structures to regulate operational principles and practices for quality assurance (personal communication, July 24, 2014). These efforts, along with the fact that the increasing participation in ELP means a corollary decrease in stigmatization, support a prognosis for growth in numbers. Grasping the weight of what that represents in terms of trends in parenting and family creation endorses the need to not just acknowledge but also intensely investigate elective lone parenting.

ELECTIVE LONE PARENTING (ELP)

Single motherhood is often bastardized through the lenses of morality and fiscal reckonings with particular class specific bias. For the financially privileged, particularly informed by conceptions of Christian womanhood, it carries a moral penalty. For the poor, economic lenses are applied, marking single motherhood as a ruse to access welfare services (Blundell et al, 2016; Herbst, 2013; Ajzenstadt, 2009; Gregg et al, 2009). For both classes, it is traditionally viewed as a consequence of irresponsible adulthood. In contrast, elective lone parenthood locates autonomy and agency in the hands of mothers. It obliterates the affiliations between motherhood and marriage, the collapsing of the identities of woman, wife, and mother, and the juxtaposition of female and male parenting identities. The distinction of wifehood for many women as merely a pathway to motherhood is clear in Oyewumi's (2000) article, where she also observes that "mother is the preferred and cherished self-identity of many African women" (p. 1096). Thus, with capacity to or compelled by circumstances to access motherhood without wifehood, ELPs alter perceptions on and of adult womanhood.

Rituals of patriarchal adult womanhood in indigenous, religious, and patriarchally inclined European and American world senses prescribe a progressive path through courtship, marriage, and then maternity (Izugbara, Ochako and Izugbara, 2011). Members of the demographic group under study in this chapter deviate from this ritualistic sequence, and do not privilege, on their journey, courtship and marriage as a pathway to motherhood. At the same time, significant expurgation of indigenous extended family modes and practices is eroding the concept of matriarchy as sanctioned by patriarchal worlds. The idea of "mother of the family" is experiencing a rebirth as this dynamic modern-day space produces a new breed of matriarchs, specifically single professional women and queer parents electively having children alone. This phenomenon, ELP, differs from single parenting. It in fact challenges the label "single parent," which often connotes a certain accidental pattern of occurrences either through accidental pregnancy, termination of a relationship, or death. ELP erases the need for a label that recognizes the absence of a second parent who is a significant other, and challenges limiting definitions of maternity and matriarchy.

The traditional characterization of matriarchy as a direct opposite of patriarchy or as delineated against an already centered patriarchy is reductive. I define matriarchy to encompass structures, organizing principles, and practices that are matrifocal, matristic, matricentric, or gylanic. Acknowledging the shifting architecture of families within middle-class Kenya, such a designation has the potential to free motherhood, and consequently matriarchy, from filters of fecundity, feminization, and sexualization in which it is frequently enframed, and the spiritual dimension of matriarchy expatiates its comprehension beyond the cosmic mother cognizance. While theorists may ponder the dialectics of defining kinship with no fathers or husbands, all non-patriarchal constructions of family including lone parenting and queer co-parenting, which represent family cultures primarily created by women, are well covered by the definition of matriarchy this chapter embraces.

Though lone mothering or parenting presents mothers independent of husband or father influence, ELP does not erase co-parenting and supportive alloparenting. To do so would be reactive to this supplementary energy, a situation that would offer the same privileging of a heterosexual male other as "necessary" for parenting. Instead, ELPs welcome a multiplicity of parenting partners, giving the proverbial statement, "it takes a village to raise a child" new and heightened meaning. In middle-class Kenya, communal parenting partners and villages, akin to those of indigenous cultures, are found in contemporary secular and religious groupings and ritualistic spaces. Many of the thirty-two SPWs who participated in this study profess that they would have preferred to have children with a partner in marriage. Indeed, six of them are divorced women who either did not have children during their first marriage or had one child and desire another. Still, the absence of such a partner does not deter those who have decided to pursue parenting. Seven who are aware that they have already lost the opportunity for direct bio-motherhood are open to other alternatives like surrogacy and adoption. Ngina shares,

> I'm not ready yet. But I am not giving up. When I tried IVF and failed, I was very broken up. I am still very broken up. I just don't think it

would be fair to bring myself like this to a child. So if I am considering adoption, which I am, I think I should deal with the pain of what I lost first before I can bring in another child. I feel like I am still in mourning for what I lost. But I have not given up. I will be a mother some day.[7]

Even with some potential lone parents reporting regret and painful experiences on their journey, expressed desire for lone parenting is still on the rise, and the women participating in this research confess to feeling empowered by their choices regardless of the outcome. ELP's rituals and negotiations empower individuals but also have the power to alter societal structures and language. Consider one woman who has an unplanned pregnancy and ends up parenting alone, and a second woman in a relationship who has a child but the relationship ends with her parenting alone. These women's situations are contemplated as happenstance. The labels attached to these two forms of coming to mothering alone are instructive. Single motherhood, as aforementioned, implies an unplanned or accidental lone parenting motherhood, often inferring an irregular parenthood. Motherhood that requires no qualification or labels occurs as part of a planned space, which translates to within a heteronormative partnership. Niara Sudarkarsa (2004), an Africanist gender scholar, in "Conceptions of Motherhood in Nuclear and Extended Families, with Special Reference to Comparative Studies Involving African Societies" expounds on this. She states, "In all human societies of which I am aware, parents are categorized as being either "married" or "unmarried" when their children are born. In other words, of all the parental attributes that might be focused on when children are born, the marital status of the parents, and particularly of the mother, is the one that is consistently considered to be relevant in many, if not most, human societies" (Sudarkarsa, 2004, p. 1).

According to Sudarkasa, the implications of this universal reality demand urgent exploration especially in today's world where models and conceptions of marriage are fast changing. One can infer from this obsession with the women's marital status that for the second woman in the scenario detailed above, while she is attached to her partner, even an abusive one, she is measured as practicing normative motherhood, which therefore requires no qualifying label. When the relationship ends, she acquires the label of single mother, and therein lies some of the power Sudarkasa alludes to. The woman acquires a label in this setup, as a single mother, suggesting that healthily parenting alone is more deviant than co-parenting in an abusive environment. These two paths to parenting alone, being "undesirable," for patriarchally inclined judgments, are short on the capacity to instigate significant transformation in how people engage gendered societal structures or view womanhood. They have agency to radically change patriarchal language and proclivities toward motherhood and womanhood, but ELP, a third atypical type of motherhood, delivers its own level of agency.

ELPs choose parenting alone and fundamentally operate without the patronage of male relatives or partners. This results in new readings of womanhood, motherhood, and matriarchy. As above-mentioned, and as Ifi Amadiume (2005) masterfully dissects it, it is simplistic to envision matriarchy as the opposite equivalent of patriarchy. A liberating definition of matriarchy concentrates on the significance of maternal codes and maternality in symbolic and practical structures of society, and disputes male-centric approaches to understanding kinship based power. This kind of perceptiveness comes to fore in observing maternal centered families, which produce their own rituals for transmitting culture, relationships, identities, lineage, family, citizenship, and ethnicity, organized and ordered along supportive matriarchal systems and praxes. One such advance is divorcing maternity from marriage. Patriarchal constructs have used fatherhood as a conduit through which to regulate girlhood, motherhood, and womanhood, ghettoizing motherhoods where a male partner is not present. Therefore, the matriarchal reconstruction delivered by father-free ELP and individual performances of non-patriarchal womanhood by ELPs negotiate new power panoramas for women as a collective.

Matriarchal readings of girlhood and womanhood prospect new roles and societal positions connected to identities housed within the generated ELP families. The creation of a family is a potent location for analyzing rituals that affect womanhood and women's power because the family space houses most significant rituals in an individual's life. Family rituals produce patterns, which through reproduction, evolve into societal culture. SPWs practice unique rituals of family creation, mostly under three cultural influences—indigenous, religious, and European and American—each offering different meaning creation opportunities and values. From the indigenous cultural perspectives, even with foreign interruptions that succeeded in creating very male-centric publics and systems, patriarchy has failed to erase the power of motherhood as demonstrated by the fact that there still exists no equivalent male space with the social, biological, and spiritual power of motherhood. It is this layered source power of the mother identity within African cultures (Kabaji, 2009; Oyewumi, 2002; Nzegwu, 2004; Pala, 2013), that ELP as a practice and experience draws from. It is important to highlight here the revolutionary epistemic potential of ELP to decenter patriarchy, by exercising the authority and supremacy inherent in motherhood that anthropologist Achola Pala (2013) expounds on in the following quote. "In Africa, motherhood is a central cosmologic concept in virtually all communities. There is a convergence in meaning of the three critical dimensions of motherhood—biological, social/economic and spiritual—that are integrally linked. Taken separately and together, the three dimensions of motherhood give women immense power, which is at times overt and at times latent" (Pala, 2013, p. 8).

Encountering and intermingling with elements of African motherhood in middle-class Kenya, are religious practices and beliefs. The convolution here is not eased by the fact that some view Christianity as a marker of modernity, and yet the secularization of Christianity through being "modern" or "contemporary" often clashes with some values ingrained in the orthodoxy of the faith. When these intricacies are overlooked, the default descriptor for the SPW is modern(ized). While European and American borrowed practices, often referred to as "modern," make up the third major influence in this scenario, such a reading is unsophisticated and equates modernization to "Westernization" raising the questions, what in fact is modern and who is a modern women? For example, is the performance of Christian religiosity and its rituals including oppressive customs toward women, modern? Even with these questions, what cannot be disputed of these women is their social standing and their relationship status, the two characteristics this chapter considers. These characteristics, along with the complex multicultural influences and resulting attitudes and practices of contemporariness, inform ELPs choices of motherhood and mothering rituals.

ELPs practice prenatal and postnatal rituals that differ from those of women getting married in that their formalities are primarily geared toward constructing a family not a relationship. A marrying woman's focus is on the relationship shared with her potential husband, while the ELPs interest is how to construct the best family and she liberally mixes indigenous, religious, and foreign customs to best serve her interests. The very process of making the choice to parent alone ritualistically involves negotiations with family and friends and other reflective, spiritual, and planning exercises. Most potential ELPs engage in parenting rituals long before they go through any procedures. Preempting challenges and the resulting apprehensions necessitate rituals of emotional and mental preparation including therapy, administering fertility medical regiments, prayers, adjusting lifestyles, and even indigenous culture medical rituals like drinking fertility portions, as three of those who participated in this study admitted to doing. All these rituals are important to the women because nervousness over the emotional cost of unsuccessful procedures is heightened by the years of investment in preparation, and failure can be traumatic, as the following quotes illustrate.

> After the first failure, I was a mess. I didn't think I could try again. I gave up. I lost the baby at almost three months. But I had one more embryo, so I had to try again. I couldn't just walk away. So I started to have hope again. I changed doctors thinking this would help. The second one didn't even take. I'm still mourning. Sometimes I wish I hadn't tried at all but I would have always wondered. It hurts." —Kui[8]

> I lost a child. Point blank. Period. I lost a child. My only child. Without ever meeting her. I think it would have been a girl.—Martha[9]

From the very beginning of their process, ELPs cognize patterns and rituals through different interactions with other women in their situation, their social support network, family, fellow church members, friends, and doctors. They have checklists of must-dos because they have to deliberately learn the rituals of an atypical parenthood. These rituals cannot be easily transmitted simply by being a part of a community where you live, observing and experiencing others mothering. For example, sperm acquisition practices and rituals that lone parenting women have to assume differ from those of women who come to parenting through rituals attached to bridehood and wifehood, or regular emotional and/or sexual relating to a partner. Potential ELPs, who use negotiated or bought sperm, are very deliberate and particular when they choose their ideal sperm mate. Carol[10] rationalizes, "I am not limited to one sperm pool, so why not pick the best?" Faith[11] adds, "I looked for super-sperm. Why not?" Some potential ELPs negotiate for sperm from acquaintances and friends. This process has its distinct rituals but also presents its own anxieties, one being that the women feel exposed and vulnerable. Negotiated sperm also complicates the space of parenting and relationships. Faith shares her process of negotiation where the men were unwilling to give up parental rights.

> Yep! I had that conversation four times; same thing over and over. I practiced it too. Then I had to change it based on the person. They are all great guys but it is not easy. I drew up a list of what I was looking for, and who met the requirements, among the men I knew. Then I had to think about whom I had the right to ask, like who was close enough to me. But I had to consider, who was married or not, what people I could trust with that information, who was mature enough to handle the conversation and so on. It takes a while just to settle on that list.

Martha relates,

> I started off with the person least likely to say no. I did not want to go down the list. I hoped it would stop with the first conversation but I was ready to have more. Number two is where I stopped. We are still talking and planning. Thankfully he was also willing to give up parental rights. If he hadn't, I would have had to move on to number three and I didn't have a number three. I would have had to start all over.

A significant number of women use the services of sperm banks in the United States, ordering from online catalogs. This trend heightens the debate on patriliny to be engaged later in this chapter. Kenya is a very classed society and sperm donation is something men with means do not dabble in openly. Additionally, indigenous societies place a lot of value on protecting lineages. Of thirty-three men from lower, middle, and upper classes asked if they would donate sperm, twenty-seven stated categorically that they would never leave "their seed" out there.[12]

Choosing a sperm donor begins the creation of a family identity informed by medical history, and balancing background information including physical attributes, temperament, career, and level of education. The decision-making and actions toward lone parenting and its rituals do not recognize and are not impacted by a significant other. The lone parent controls expedition on a journey of choice by one unattached parent. Therefore, a comprehension of ELPs and the transformative location they occupy begins with recognizing the ludicrousness of the label "single mother."

The concept of single motherhood is, as referenced earlier in the chapter, contested by Oyewumi who critiques the failure of feminist literature that continues the practice of subsuming motherhood under wifehood (2002, p. 5). Referencing mothers as single misrepresents the nature of the relationship between mothers and children, and erases the plethora of conceptualizations of African motherhood captured in Achola Pala's explication that follows. Pala informs that motherhood, conceptually or by name, is not limited in definition, or by biology, or legitimated by marriage (p. 8). She explains that "An African woman is a mother by virtue of the power vested in her class (social category) as one who possesses a reproductive and nurturing responsibility and quality" (p. 8). The term "single mother," ambiguous in its meaning, erases significant properties and forms of mothering and motherhood, and with that, conceptual frameworks for relating to womanhood and parenthood. Its sexualization of motherhood, which reduces it to a phenomenon that exists within a conjugal arrangement, and the stigma of the tag "single mother" contribute directly to delayed motherhood that sometimes leads to denied motherhood for many women. This is the experience of many Kenyan SPWs. A term bearing no meaning is thus imbued with substantive control over the institution of motherhood and family, and consequently, the identity, woman. The very stigma that may have contributed to some women's choice to delay motherhood until they have a partner, ironically, originates their choice of elective lone parenting.

SPWs pursuing ELP are not necessarily out to deliberately make a political statement, yet their choices and rituals are singularities worthy of analysis to inform the changing conceptions of family, motherhood, and womanhood. As women step into this form of parenting, they are by default triggering new identities within families. The identities that result defy mainstream conceptions of lineage founding and kinship among Kenyan communities. Sudarkasa depicts African family forms as flexible enough to accommodate new units and emerging forms, jettisoning notions of strictly packaged patri-lineages. She sums up the extended family across African cultures not as an extension of the conjugal family unit but one that is built around a lineage, and allows for other familial units to exist within it (Sudarkasa, 2004, pp. 3–4). Per this understanding, new family variants in contemporary Kenya, like ELP families, that can accommodate new blood lines, fit into the extended family form, as explicated in the next section.

The Challenge to Patriliny

The performance of motherhood identities by ELPs transforms conceptions of womanhood particularly for societies that are identified primarily as patrilocal, patrilineal, and patriarchal. The necessary jump off position in contemplating contemporary Kenyan families bearing indigenous, religious, and European and American influences is in fact a consideration of patriliny and patriarchy. Because the family unit is a microcosm of the larger society, and the basic unit of its organization, changes in the structural alignment within the family unit induce change in structures, roles, and location of bodies and power at a societal level. ELP refashions compositions and constructions of family. In Kenya, because most societies, indigenous and contemporary, remain patriarchal (Sanya, 2013; Maseno and Kilonzo, 2011; Hussein, 2009; Kariuki, 2006), such restructuring affects the patriarchal paradigms that accompany the foundation of families.

Parenting rituals of ELPs produce family interfaces, which yield a community—including social fathers and mothers—not beholden to patriarchal regulations or to patrilines. In this way, they defy culturally endorsed interference rights bestowed on male relatives in Christian, European and American, and indigenous communities. The mother controls in what ways the child is an insider or outsider in the circles she chooses for her family. In many Kenyan cultures, in the absence of a father, the other fathers, who are often brothers of the father, step in. This is the equivalent of an uncle in the European or American world. In the world sense of many Kenyan communities, this is a complex identity. The brother of one's father is, in fact, a father not an uncle. Thus, fatherhood is transferred in the absence of the bio-father. The bloodline shared between a father and his male siblings allows for them to step in as father-stand-ins, a role assured by lineage. With ELP, there is no fatherhood to be transferred because no bloodline recognized father exists socially or biophysically, whether in the process of adoption, surrogacy, or IVF. In ELP, there are social fathers and uncles present, and some of these are invited males that may not be related by blood to the mother. The power here rests not within a bloodline but with the mother who establishes and so can revoke the offer of the relationship. The lone parent legalizes and legitimates family status not just for the child but also for friends and relatives. The father-uncle tag therefore encompasses invited males who range from friends to relatives. Usually, those social fathers and uncles are welcomed into the child's life because they belong to the mother's networks and are her equals in the social and career world and so there is no power differential between them. Patriarchal policing is interrupted when male relatives do not have bloodline-sanctioned rights to opinion and influence.

Bloodline legitimated male authority is taken for granted across many Kenyan families and communities, which are patrilineal. The narratives of ELPs raise a series of compelling questions that must force an interrogation and reconsideration of constructs of patriliny. Is biologized patriliny[13] erased when knowledge of the sperm donor or father of adopted child is unavailable? When the sperm donor or father is known but not acknowledged as family, is patriliny likewise erased? Does the child parented alone bear the lineage of the mother, that of his mother's father, or begin his own lineage? Can the mother be passed over to re-assign the role of lineage founder to a male to maintain the status quo of patriliny? The question of assigning lineage takes on greater novelty with IVF and surrogacy when one considers distant biologized lineage, for example with sperm ordered from laboratories in the United States. In all these cases, the mother's is the only culturally situated lineage, often the only accessible or identifiable one. In a patrilineal society, which privileges male blood lineage, since she is not a man who carried forth her own father's lineage, she must be recognized as beginning a matrilineal descent line. If her community only recognizes a patrilineal bloodline, then she effectually starts a line outside of the community's lineage system and this affirms ELPs' location as a lineage founder. With numbers of ELPs set to rise, allowances must be made for women carrying forward bloodlines within the communities' understandings and considerations for family generational transmission.

Beyond definitions of bloodlines, ELP also changes the traditional understanding of family through a re-invention of the nature and function of rituals such as naming. These rituals traditionally sustain patriarchal organizing and affirm agnatic kinship. In this instance, however, rituals that the mother privileges like choice of family name or child's name allow for the definition of a social family location for the child. With no father physically present, certain cultural requirements for the child to take the father's or his relatives' names may be discarded. Rituals of naming children after certain relatives, mostly from the father's side of the family from indigenous cultures, as well as the European and American practice of having a family name attached to the father are both disrupted. The name an elective lone parent uses is usually natally located, her last name, which is sometimes also her father's name. However, this is not to be confused with passing on her father's lineage. In mothering under patriliny, adopting the family name re-affirms patriarchy as an organizing principle. In the case of ELP, the name the child takes may be shared with the natal family but the mother carries the bloodline forward. The shared name serves the purpose of allowing the child to belong as part of a collective, offering a social location or identity for the child. If ELPs are recognized as founders of lineages, then communities in which these women live cannot be referenced as decisively patrilineal, and sub-segments of Kenyan communities traditionally viewed as patrilineal must be redefined as multilineal, duo-lineal, or bilineal.

In parts of Kenya's history, lineage and legitimacy have been linked. The British Parliament in 1926 passed the Legitimacy Ordinance, recognizing "illegitimate" children who could be legitimated by the marriage of their parents. This would be adjusted and adopted by the Kenyan Legislative Council (Thomas, 2003, p. 138). Years later, its language and spirit persist in collective social psyche. So what elective lone parents are doing is redefining legitimate motherhood and fatherhood, challenging the patriarchal paradigm that mothers can have illegitimate children while fathers cannot. Legally recognized and legitimated, they further validate their family and socially locate their children through the performance of a series of rituals like portraiture, church baptisms, and indigenous naming and shaving ceremonies. For adoptive mothers, Gotcha! celebrations borrowed from the United States ritualize birth and family creation. These rituals sometimes are premeditated to protect patrimony on behalf of the child within their natal family, a concern that also motivates some mothers to embrace their own father's lineage as some have shared.

> I would want my child to belong to something larger than me. —Lucy[14]
>
> I would have wanted her to have a right to her inheritance from the extended family so I would have held onto the lineage. —Martha

Yet, for the same reason that Martha submits for her preference, some of the women interviewed warmed up to the idea of the establishment of a new lineage, as indicated in the quotes that follow.

> I am not married. If anything happened to me, these crazy patriarchy people could take everything from my child. You have seen how they go after property when someone dies. —Josephine[15]
>
> Wow! Now that I think about it, is there any way to make this lineage founder thing legal? That way I would be sure for sure that my child's rights were forever protected. My best friend is a lawyer and single like me. I intend to have my kid's rights firmly sealed. However, after you are gone these people can do you in and do some stuff you never imagined would happen. I saw it happen to my mother when my dad passed on. —Carol

Extrication from the lineage while still enjoying the social benefits of community that an extended family provides is easily supported by the fact that urban existence is not dependent on communal living, which was necessary in ancestral family compounds in indigenous communities (Kenyatta, 2015; Adams and Mburugu, 1994; Gunga, 2009). Urban Kenyans generate new villages embedded in their Christian and secular social publics. This space can dynamically receive and accommodate new matrilineal families and matriarchies like the ones led by ELPs. This is the new societal structure being engendered in Kenya's middle class. A mother lineage that is supported within a larger clan is more likely to survive independently while at the same time benefitting from and contributing to the community provided by the extended family unit. The kinship based family structure, considered per Sudakarsa's (2004) definition, need not be disrupted by recognition of matrilineal pockets within Kenyan communities. Further, de-gendering the concept head of household aids the project of differentiating between a family and a household, and flexibility toward incorporating new family structures and value systems uncommitted to gender.

CONCLUSION

In this chapter I have undertaken an examination of motherhood and womanhood in contemporary times through an analysis of how a specific sub-set of women navigate and perform parenthood and parenting. How these women traverse the challenges, stake, and agency of their space of motherhood, absent or present, is challenging and rewriting societal scripts previously anchored in patrilineal standards. Because patriliny is attached to and informs patriarchy, the result is a contestation of patriarchal principles and the related people identities. Contemporary Kenyan mothers, considered monolithically, traditionally respond to three spaces, all patriarchally constructed—religious, indigenous cultural spaces, and spaces attached to foreign borrowed cultures and influences. Socially acceptable practices of motherhood and womanhood are typically informed by these hegemonic patriarchal value systems. Alternatives to male-centric conceptions of family and kinship, like ELP, allow for an acknowledgment of successful modern matrilineages and matriarchies, and new matrilineal spaces have monumental implications for the location of women in society.

Middle-class Kenya's cleavages of matriliny and matriarchy contest androcracy through questioning patriliny's social significance to motherhood, and the subsuming of motherhood within patriarchally constructed family and societal structures. With women circumventing the marriage portal, the centrality of wifehood is eroded particularly in relation to its significance to motherhood. Mary O'Brien in *The Politics of Reproduction* argues that men needed patriarchy to address their paternal anxiety because they lack certainty about paternity (1981, pp. 54–61). As the saying goes, only the mother truly knows who the father of a child is. Patriarchally constructed virtuous motherhood, housed within a heterosexual marriage mitigated this fear for men. Lone parenting mothers offer a parenthood not beholden to serving patriarchal and paternal anxiety. The result is a motherhood that is as autonomous as fatherhood—a womanhood independent from manhood.

Intent and value systems are manifest through actions, in this case rituals attached to motherhood and contemporary adult womanhood sans wifehood. As scholarship continues to engage womanhood and motherhood in terms of tools, laws, traditions, rituals, customs, education, language, and labor, it is important to pay attention to elective lone parents because in terms of changing the terrain of family, they occupy one of the most powerful loci. Understanding how they manipulate their place to occasion the redistribution of privilege and power is important for any political, social, economic, or cultural projects or initiatives, as well as any scholarship, directed at the Kenyan family.

NOTES

1. Dr. Patel is a professor at the Aga Khan University Hospital. He is a consultant obstetrician and gynecologist at the Kenya Fertility, I.V.F., and ICSI Center. He is one of the most sought after assisted reproductive technology (ART) specialists in the country.

2. Dr. Noreh is the lead clinical embryologist, gynecologist, medical director, and obstetrician at the Nairobi IVF Center. He is one of the most sought after assisted reproductive technology (ART) specialists in the country.

3. Adoption and legal fees compound the burden of expenses for medication, procedures, day to day care of the surrogate mother, and the high fees paid to the surrogate mother for services rendered. Because most surrogates come from poor backgrounds and the care of the unborn child, including nutrition and healthcare, could be compromised, women host their surrogates for the duration of the pregnancy. Dr. Patel shares that the doctors often advise women to host their surrogates so they can monitor and support the best progression of the pregnancy.

4. This figure was offered by calculations from Dr. Patel's practice. He explained that this was on the conservative end of the scale and did not take into account repeat procedures in the event of procedural failure. This figure is the equivalent of between $20,000 and $25,000 US dollars depending on the exchange rate.

5. While an elective lone parent does not have to engage in rituals of wifehood, with parenthood expanded in definition and responsibilities, she does have to develop rituals of reconciling career and family life. Terry, whose circumstances have not changed from what stopped her participation in bio-motherhood in the first place shares, "I'm still busy. I'm actually busier than I was before. I'm a director now. So what has changed? I have come a long way and I'm not sure I could just so easily give it all up, and I think I would have to if I had a child alone. Don't get me wrong. I want children. If I could clone myself, I would be at the IVF clinic right now." The interviews with Terry, whose name has been changed to protect her privacy were conducted on the 5th and 6th of July 2014.

6. Nduta is forty-four-years-old. She is co-owner of an advertising firm in Nairobi. The interviews with Nduta, whose name has been changed to protect her privacy, were conducted in Nairobi on 25th July 2014.

7. Ngina is a marketing manager with the Kenya office of a multinational company. Interviews with Ngina, whose name has been changed to protect her privacy were conducted in Lavington, Nairobi, on the 5th and 6th of July 2014.

8. Kui is a forty-five-year-old professor. The interviews with Kui, whose name has been changed to protect her identity, were conducted via e-mail between the 20th and the 30th of June 2014.

9. Martha is a forty-six-year-old media executive. The interviews with Martha, whose name has been changed to protect her privacy, were conducted in Riara, Nairobi, on the 4th of July 2014.

10. Carol is a medical practitioner. The interviews with Carol, whose name has been changed to protect her privacy, were conducted in Riara, Nairobi, on the 2nd of July 2014.

11. Skype interview. The interviews with Faith, whose name has been changed to protect her privacy, were conducted on the 5th of February 2015.

12. At casual conversations and e-mail exchanges with thirty-three men over the period of three years, responses to the question of whether they would serve as sperm donors were collected. The question, mostly, returned a resounding, "No!" Seven of the men stated that they would serve as sperm donors for friends if they were allowed to be part of the children's lives. Five of the seven were married and so stated that this would get in the way of their willingness to serve as sperm donors.

13. Nkiru Nzegwu (2004b) in "The Epistemological Challenge of Motherhood to Patriliny" argues that biologized patriliny is rooted solely in biological fatherhood and ignores social patriliny rooted in social fatherhood. She further argues that scholars who privilege this definition of patriliny conflate patriliny and patriarchy.

14. Lucy is a forty-eight-year-old adoptive mother of one. The interviews with Lucy, whose name has been changed to protect her privacy, were conducted in Lavington, Nairobi, on 14th July 2013.

15. Josephine is a self-employed business woman and employer. Interviews with Josephine, whose name has been changed to protect her privacy, were conducted in Kilimani, Nairobi, on the 20th of June 2015.

TWO

Usichana wa Ubabi

Erasures of Ritual and the Myth of Independence

Dean and Laidler (2013) demonstrate that, "female adolescence is typically a highly controlled and managed process, with considerable social pressure being applied to ensure that girls safely transition into normative womanhood" (2009, para. 5). In most cultures globally, including those of Kenya, adults have traditionally constructed girlhood. Girl cultures are fundamentally always fast evolving, and among present day Kenya's middle class, such evolution appears to lack rootedness in any specific culture, suggesting a lack of standard systems through which adults or society can formally aid the production of girlhood. Karanja (2010) points to this hybridized nature of the youth identity in urban Kenya as a contributing factor to the "dilemma, ambivalence, and contradiction" they experience in attempting a navigation of an urban culture with multiple external and indigenous influences (p. 10). Significant to the changes in practices and habits of Kenyan girls that accompany this active intercourse of influences, both materially and in relation to values, is the loss of particularities of different indigenous Kenyan communities.

Many middle-class Kenyan girls, especially those living in urban areas, have little interaction with the traditions of their indigenous communities. Many do not speak indigenous languages that would allow them access to indigenous ways of knowing and being. More and more, younger Kenyans' understanding of indigenous cultures and values is limited to two things—food and respect for one's elders—and even that, in the era of individualism and "independence," they do not necessarily practice. Forty-two girls in Nairobi, Kisumu, Eldoret, Thika, and Mombasa between the ages of fourteen and nineteen, representing Akamba, Luhya, Gikuyu, Kalenjin, and Luo communities, offered three aspects of their indigenous cultures they were familiar with: food, respect for elders, and folklore they learned about in literature classes (January 21, 2017). None were able to offer knowledge of any specific cultural rituals or practices from their indigenous communities. This indeed is noted as a marker of *ubabi*.[1] As *wasichana wababi*, girls from Babylon, they exist in multi-cultural realities, and with Hollywoodization, the Internet, and social media, European and American ways are handy and do become the primary informing cultures in the choice of lifestyles, languages, adornments, habits and rituals.

Dean and Laidler (2013) advance that with girls increasingly finding their social interactions primarily online, and contributing to the creation and dissemination of cultures online, it is imperative that society and scholars inquire into the impact of this expanded social world for girls (para. 13). Online cultures and popular culture have a way of highlighting segments of culture that may be disregarded in formal representations of a society (Ligaga, 2010, p. 1), and common affinities with Kenyan girl cultures observed in social and other popular media productions reproduce the patterns that appear to celebrate Americanness with a sprinkling of European practices and philosophies. A question to forty-two teenagers between the ages of thirteen and nineteen revealed that their favorite musicians or music groups, movies, celebrities, and fashion brands, were all American with a smattering of European selections. The rising embrace of local popular artists by Kenyan youth is in part because these artists mimic Hollywood entertainers and celebrities in performing styles as well as lifestyle. In Kenya, especially among the young middle class, the abandonment of indigenous and religious rituals has increasingly become both an indicator of progressiveness and a badge of elitism.

Based on the foregoing, one could argue that the desire for Europeanization and Americanization contests the argument for an absence of loyalty to any one culture. This would be plausible if Kenyans had societally recognized custodians and adjudicators of American and European cultures. The absence of such overseers eliminates the compulsory and obligatory aspect, as well as definition of standard expectations for performing Americanness or Europeanness. Still, for Kenyan middle-class girls, global influences sustained through new media advancements cannot be completely alleviated (O'Keefe and Clarke-Pearson, 2011; Lenhart, Purcell, Smith, and Zickuhr, 2010; Barker, 2009). Dialogues on modern girlhood must consider ways in which virtual social spaces are rewriting girlhoods (Dean and Laidler, 2013). These new frontiers of human interaction and performance demand new imaginations of cognition, and so new measures for the construction and development of girlhoods.

Technology and real-time access to information, people, and services from across the globe require that the individual's development and skill mastery include capacity to locate oneself within, and competently participate in a technology driven world. This reconstruction of performances of girlhood, in some ways, places the girls' cognitive development ahead of that of their supervising adults. The resulting scenario centers new actors as primary influencers of girls' rituals. Asked the question, "Where do you get most of your information?" three focus groups of middle-class girls offered responses that support this argument. Of thirty-six girls between the ages of thirteen and eighteen who participated, an overwhelming thirty-three indicated receiving lifestyle and life skill lessons from online sources including Pinterest, Instagram, Youtube, Facebook groups, Whatsapp groups, and other social media as well as regular web pages. All thirty-six received news and information from their peers. While they all still received guidance from parents and other adults, more than fifty percent confessed to privileging what they received from their peers more than adults when it came to their social lives and the creation of girl cultures. They contend that parents almost always give them information they "already know." The results from the focus groups bear out results collected from individual conversations with girls across the country during the period of this research.

With unlimited borders to knowledge acquisition, and loss of control by extended family, girls appear to be shifting institutional dynamics, and temporalities—often leading to moral panic among adults. Attempting to reconcile frictions and tensions occasioned by the loss of religious and indigenous anchors in modern girlhood presents new anxieties especially for parents. As Ngele explained, "I only have to sit at the mall, eating my ice cream and watching the thirteen-going-on-thirty-something girls to fear for my little one. And she is not even close to teenage!"(personal communication, July 29, 2014).

In this chapter, I focus on the demographic of females between the ages of thirteen and nineteen for a number of reasons. First, this is the stage on the continuum of girlhood and womanhood where establishing independence is expected. At this age, questions of identity and visibility become important as girls start to consider their own self-representation and selfhood within group cultures (Mitchell and Reid-Walsh, 2005; Vares, Jackson, and Gill, 2011). Among Kenya's middle class, typically, activities of toddlers and preschoolers, and early school going girls are attached to supervised spaces within and outside the home. Unlike generations before them who enjoyed free unsupervised play, middle-class Kenyan little girls fill up their social time with teacher, counselor, parent or nanny supervised school and recreational activities. While their counterparts from less affluent neighborhoods or the rural areas detach from constant handling and monitoring sooner, unmonitored interactions with the larger world emerge later for middle-class girls during what are commonly referred to as the teen years.

Another reason for focusing on coming-of-age girlhood is that this book's interest is girlhoods and womanhoods. This makes coming-of-age significant precisely because it sits at the cusp of transitioning from girlhood to womanhood. Coming of age, the young person encounters the adult world, confronts moral challenges and awakenings as well as weighs individual needs against external expectations and norms. There is a loss of innocence as one begins the journey of encountering the world as a complex place, comes face-to-face with personal limitations, and is thrust into a way of interacting with the world rooted more in realism than idealism (Kroger, 2004; Huffaker and Calvert, 2005; Hall and Brown-Thirston, 2011). This transition from girlhood to womanhood demands rituals that mark the crossover in what is expected to be a process of maturing.

Maturity implies asserting independence, and so I raise and respond, in this chapter, to questions instigated by two suppositions. The first one is that coming-of-age is a liberating process that initiates the individual's independence, and increases their value as a functioning contributing member of society. The second assumption is that a lack of indigenous culture and religious pressures and oversight among twenty-first century Kenya's middle class has resulted in greater autonomy for girls who appear to have the freedom to create their own coming-of-age rituals. The assumed transformation in ideas and practices toward "modern" living of the middle class suggests that, for girls, this represents an unbound coming of age process anchored in "new age" unconventionality and individualism. I interrogate these postulations through an examination of the effects of adapting English terminology to reference Kenyan girls and girlhood stages, the resulting erasure of rituals, as well as the restrictions to coding of the self within middle-class social institutions. I advance arguments on how these developments have compromised the performativity of the concept and phrase "coming-of-age." I am not interested, in this work, in problematizing specific rituals and activities of girls, and will not be debating morality or advocating proper girlhoods. I also refrain from foregrounding rituals of "gendered" parenting because this is not the focus of this chapter. Additionally, among the middle class in Kenya, by degrees, there is an observable decrease in gendered parenting.

Just Girls?: Limitations of the English Language

Driscoll (2008) accurately states that if the concept culture is as hard to pin down in definition as the category "girl," then the definition of "girl cultures" is necessarily a convoluted endeavor (p. 28). I kick off the arguments of this chapter by highlighting the complications attached to using "girl" as a moniker capturing the expansive ages of one to eighteen. The limitations of this single word in theorizing, and even naming, become glaring as one attempts to particularize in analysis aspects of the different stages of girlhood. The subcategories of girlhood into stages like the tween and the teen have been developed to manage this complexity in

English, with tweenage covering about three years preceding the teen years (Driscoll, 2008, p. 24), and in the past, before adolescence. However groupings like adolescents, young women, or tweens and teens are restricted in their usefulness by the fact that adolescence, tweenage, and teenage are used more to define and construct age delineating factors rather than sex particularizing cultures and behaviors, especially contextualized within specific cultures across the globe. Durham (2015) parallels the stages "teenage" and "childhood" as "social artifacts" and not "biological categories," explicating that they are sociocultural constructions that differentiate their character from adulthood (p. 506). Equally constructed, tweenage as a category was originated in the late twentieth century by consumer media upon the realization that this demographic was commercially lucrative (Brookes and Kelly, 2009, p. 600).

Complicating this scenario further is the fact that the lines between the tweenage and teenage girls are becoming increasingly blurred not just in terms of rituals and cultures including language, fashion, pop culture interests, but also in terms of biology. Some studies indicate that girls are maturing earlier biologically (Brown, Halpern and L'Engle, 2005; Steingraber, 2007; Kaplowitz, 2011). This muddies the definition of preadolescent and adolescent years in terms of numbered age. For girls, early puberty forces attempts at early psychological and social maturity (Brown et al.; Deardorff, 2005; James, Ellis, Schlomer and Garber, 2012; Kaltiala-Heino, Kosunen, and Rimpela, 2003). What teenage and tweenage become, therefore, are numbers of ages that have little descriptive value for not just the performance of, but also essentially the being-ness of girlhood.

Indigenous Kenyan communities appreciate(d) the limitations of defining stages of girlhood based on years of living. They outline different stages of girlhood based on more than just a number in age. Of the twelve educators and scholars of culture from different Kenyan communities interviewed for this chapter, not one could offer an answer to the question, "When does girlhood end in terms of numbered age?" None of the scholars defined girlhood stages as a function of age. Their definitions consider developments, roles, relationships, and responsibilities. Among the Gikuyu, philosopher and gender scholar Betty Wambui in her chapter, "*Kūgeria Mīario: Atumia, Ciana, Mbūri, Mīgūnda*," translated by Evan Mwangi, as "Conversations: Women, Children, Goats, Land," explains that, "within age-sets, people took various steps as they grew up. A female baby (*mwana*) would grow into a *kairītu* (girl). After some years, she grew into a *kīrīgū*—an older adolescent girl who is not yet circumcised. After circumcision, a female became a *mūiritu*. After circumcision and marriage, a female became a *mūtumia* (a married woman)" (Wambui, 2013, p. 97).

Literary and gender studies scholars Evan Mwangi and Wangui wa Goro offer further clarifications about the Gikuyu age defining system, conceptualizing an outline that is about more than a number (online communications, September 27, 2016). Other Kenyan communities conceived girlhood analogously. Performance and cultural studies and gender studies scholar Mshai Mwangola defines Taita girlhood and womanhood thus. A female person is *"mjighe* (little girl) once you grew out of being a baby (*mwana*) then *mwai.*" Mwangola elucidates that, "There is no equivalent in English for *mwai* but the closest comparative state would be "maiden," once your menses come. [One is] *mwai* until one gets married because then you become a woman, *mka*" (online communication, August 26, 2016). Among the Akamba, the naming of boyhood appears more invested in than that of girls. *Kelitu* designates a small girl while *mwilitu* is a big girl, similar to the Gikuyu *muiritu*. A much bigger girl is *iilitu*. A small boy is *kavisi*, a boy without diminution or augmentation is *kivisi*, while a big boy is *ivisi*. A male youth, the equivalent of numbered age system's fifteen- to twenty-four-year old is referred to as *mwanake* (Mumo Kasamba, personal communication, January 16, 2017).

In the classifications above, the interviewees rarely used the word "older" in relation to numbered age. Rather, the world "small" or "big" are used. The small and big can thus refer to age as well as size and capacity to manage age appropriate responsibilities in referencing girls. Still, words like *muiritu* or *mwilitu*, among the Gikuyu and Akamba, respectively, are typically not used to reference a girl pre-puberty no matter what physical size they are. These words are therefore more significantly a reference to stages of maturity than size or numbered age. Wangui wa Goro shares that among the Gikuyu, "the distinctions of girlhood and womanhood [are]: "younger/younger young/young/older/older/adult" (online interview, September 27, 2016). It is in an attempt to capture these layers that one encounters the limitations of English language terminologies. I illustrate this further by testing the numbered age system employed today in signifying girlhood against the Wanga Luhya and Luo cultural conceptualizations.

Cultural educationist Francis Lutomia offers a very precise system of naming girlhood among the Wanga of Western Kenya. Generally, a girl is called *omukhana*. Conceptually, *omukhana* refers to a young female, not yet married and not yet a bio-mother. The Wanga meticulously delineate different stages of girlhood and the English language fails at reproducing these classifications. *Lishere* is a girl one hour to one day old. From infancy to six months, all children, regardless of sex, are *tsindana*, after which, the female child is just *omwana omukhana*. From ages one to about ten years old, she becomes simply *omukhan*a. Between eleven and fourteen years old, pre-adolescence, she is *omukhana omuvukha*. Once, at puberty, as her body begins to transform, she is referred to as *mkhana afumure tsimbere,* a girl who has developed breasts. Post the onset of adolescence, she becomes *omukhana ali mlukhana lwa mbeli*, one in the first/early stages of girlhood or first stage of coming-of-age. Once she is considered mature and ready for marriage she is referred to as *omukhana ali mlukhana lwa khavili,* one in the second stages of girlhood or second stage of coming-of-age, or *omukhana imbiji*. The word *omukhana,* can however be used in other ways. Fathers and mothers may call their daughters *omukhana* at any age as a term of endearment and respect. *Abakhasi,* married women, may be referred to as *omukhana* in the following ways. *Omukhana* Navaleka—this would be a title given to a clanswoman of the Navaleka clan, *omundu wo luhya*—a person (member) of the clan at any age. When describing a female member from a certain clan you indicate the designation *omukhana* and then the clan name, for example, *omukhana* Navaleka, *omukhana* Bwibo, *omukhana* Ngakhwa, *or omukhana* Luleti. This is often used to confer value and admiration to her and the people she hails from (F. Lutomia, personal communications, October 2016). Navaleka, Bwibo, Ngakhwa and Luleti are clan names.

Anthropologist Achola Pala, in the following, elaborates on the Luo conceptualization of girlhood.

> In Dholuo, *nyako* means a prepubescent girl or not yet married young woman. Strictly speaking a prepubescent girl may be referred to as *nyathi manyako,* meaning what has now come to be referred to as the girl child. A young woman—post adolescent—who may be of marriageable age is called *nyako*. Sociolinguistically one might say that *nyako* is a diminutive of *dhako* the term used to refer to a mature married woman. *Nyako* also implies that the young woman is not a child and is of legal marriage age, and capable of producing a baby, biologically speaking (personal communication, October 5, 2017).

The prefix "nya-" in Dholuo usually captures the concept "smaller in stature or younger in age." *Dhako maduong* is a more mature woman of middle age. This term may, however, not be applied to a middle-aged woman who is not married. She would be called *nyako* until marriage or once she graduates further in age, hence *dhako moti,* a mature old woman, post-menopausal. Dr. Pala explains further that, "a woman can be called *nyako* even when she is married, middle aged, or old as a term of endearment and usually by her age mates or men with whom she shares a joking relationship—especially brothers-in–law" (personal communication, October 5, 2016).

The foregoing clarifies the complexity of the identity "girl" and that the designation of age is about more than a number, thus the practice of maintaining age sets, which consisted of people with a range of close numbered ages in many African cultures. Macharia (2012) locates girlhood as a social event, indicating that peer groups formed through performing the rituals of girlhood endured throughout life (p. 6). These scholars and educationists, referencing different Kenyan communities, define age as a set of qualities including number of years, knowledge and skills development, biological development, relationship status, and roles earned through social education and rituals. A failure to reconcile new definitions of girlhood in adapted languages like English with different cultural practices and conceptualizations of girlhood in Kenya has occasioned what appears to be a non-defined and non-directed coming-of-age girlhood. The adoption of the numbered age as a definer of stages of girlhood and womanhood means that at eighteen, one unequivocally and uncontestably becomes an adult. The implication here is that no preparation is required toward adulthood. Coming-of-age therefore is no longer a process but a state assured by a set of numbers.

In contemporary Kenya, most communities have espoused the legal definition that marks all ages between one and eighteen as girlhood, and at eighteen, the girl simply and automatically becomes a woman even though no universal understanding of the start of adulthood exists (Sawyer, Afifi, Bearinger, Blakemore, Dick, Ezeh, and Patton, 2012) and the "adolescent brain continues to mature well into the 20s" (Johnson, Blum, and Giedd, 2009, p. 216). This age, though not scientifically supported, is legally accepted, and is developmentally arbitrary (Johnson et al., p. 217). Even in countries where it was first adopted, it is riddled with complications. For example in the United States, an eighteen-year-old "woman" can serve in the military but an eighteen-year-old teenager is not old enough, legally, to drink alcohol. The very numbering itself also yields confusion. A nineteen year old is legally an adult but still a teenager, and teenagers are more often than not viewed as more children than adults. The adaptation by Kenyans of this legal definition of girlhood did not incorporate a consideration for biological, psychological, social or cultural factors offered by indigenous thought systems. Following colonialism, the remnants of indigenous cultural considerations in conceptualizing age lingered for a while among the middle class, but the current generation of teens and tweens is perhaps historically the most removed from such structuring of girlhood.

This reality, for middle-class children, which ensures automatic unearned coming to adulthood makes rituals of coming-of-age pointless. With that is a seeming acceptance of girls controlling their own processes of coming-of-age, and so perhaps the perception of assured early independence for girls from societally monitored coming-of-age. In the next section I examine this claim of independence.

Erasure of Ritual and the Myth of Independence

It is imperative to note here that in referencing initiation, analysis, or problematization of genital modification is beyond the scope of this work. Mentions of coming-of-age rituals do not cover any type of genital or other body modifications, but instead references made here are to lessons and conversations of coming-of-age processes. I acknowledge that in some communities in Kenya, genital cutting was a part of the initiation process. However, my interest here is in the non-cutting equivalents of initiation rituals that framed coming-of-age—the knowledge and skill acquisition processes. Even in societies with genital modification practices, coming-of-age rites went beyond the cutting (Munthali and Zulu, 2007).

Across cultures, coming-of-age has historically been the first and most recognized rite of passage for females. It is an extended ritual experience involving a period of liminality. The late tween and early teen years serve as the preliminal ritualistic stage. Next comes the liminal stage where the young one is neither girl nor woman but, in English, is referred to as girl until they magically cross over into adulthood at eighteen. Richard Schechner's definition of the three stages of a ritual event can be applied here. He states, "during the liminal phase of a ritual, two things are accomplished: First, those undergoing the ritual temporarily become "nothing," put into a state of extreme vulnerability where they are open to change." Schechner expounds further that "During the liminal phase, the work of rites of passage take place. At this time, in specially marked spaces, transitions and transformations occur." He adds, "Persons are stripped of their former identities and positions in the formal world [. . .] in the midst of a journey from one social self to another" (Schechner, 2013, p. 66).

As an experience, coming-of-age is an extended active ritual, and within it specific rituals preparing girls for adulthood among Kenya's different indigenous communities including the Luhya, Gikuyu, Luo, and Kalenjin were elaborate. This process of finding autonomy was particularly embraced by the wealthy in society who self-presented as the custodians and perfect representatives of the community's values and norms. They could also afford every ritual, and used such opportunities to parade their wealth. Coming-of-age is an identity of process, the process of nascent adulthood, and so it is an unfixed condition. Among Kenya's middle class today, what has replaced the rituals of indigenous communities is unclear, and in scholarship there is a glaring absence of studies on the performance of girlhood or what represents the graduation from girlhood to womanhood. The erasure of rituals that are a part of the process leaves little as a starting point for any study. Quasi-replacement practices including confirmation in certain Christian faiths belong to the tween and pre-tween years and only cover symbolic religious maturing (Jarvis, 2007, p. 84).

A few middle-class families, particularly in Nairobi, over the past decade have started hosting simulations of parts of indigenous initiation rituals for coming-of-age girls. These typically include elegant and elaborate events for girls and their parents and other sponsors where they receive teachings and advice on girlhood, womanhood, and adulthood. Such counsel is tailored to their current world, and to middle-class ways of appreciating success, relationships, and family. This new trend is indicative of an expanding recognition of gaps in the socialization of young people. Florence, a mother of a fourteen-year-old girl shares: "It is hard to watch some of these litu pipo (little people). They are missing out on any guidance at all. You try at home but the media and their peers are pushing their own agenda. So, parents are realizing that formalizing the teachings as an event may help, you know, like our ancestors did" (personal communication, June 13, 2015).

A majority of middle class Kenyans do not mark this significant passage into a different phase of life in any way, leaving the young ones uninformed on the shifting expectations of society and their new location and roles. In this way, their understanding of adulting is limited to acquiring social and financial freedom. Initiation rituals in practices of indigenous cultures expedited a smooth transition from girlhood to pre-womanhood, and eventually womanhood. These rituals marked, for girls, a shift as part of an age-set, complete with societal role transition, and so it transcribed to the youth the implications of their transference into adulthood. Today, with this message not communicated as a function of the erasure of symbolic rituals and ceremonies, teenagers assume that independence only means lack of interference in their activities. Asked about the ubiquitous phrase teenagers use, "I am not a child," fifteen- and sixteen-year-old members of a focus group offered different versions of the same response. They explain their purpose, which is to communicate that they should be monitored less and trusted to make their own decisions.

All thirty-six girls in the focus groups expressed a desire for this kind of independence from their families and communities (focus groups, May 16–18, 2016). They neglected and struggled with committing to the idea that responsibility to a community makes independence and indeed maturity conditional, and that independence is affirmed through exercising emotional, financial, and intellectual self-sufficiency. Authentic and realistic maturity and independence is signaled by implicit and active selfhood and autonomy, and involves acquiring a level of self-reliance. Such a definition challenges the project of twenty-first century coming-of-age social independence resulting from simplistic envisioning of maturity as freedom from family "interference," or what I refer to as vanity resistances that serve only unsophisticated self-interests.

The sense of false emancipation among girls is an outcome, in part, of society's failure to offer adequate aid to teenagers through the coming-of-age processes. Unguided and floundering through coming-of-age uncertainties, girls imagine themselves acquiring more autonomy because without context that expounds on their new identities, or what it means to not be a child any more, they are reminded often that they are no longer children. Twenty-seven of thirty-three mothers and fathers interviewed confessed to using this phrase when reprimanding or advising their teenagers. The coming-of-age girls internalize this message and repeat it often in demanding adult treatment, but without the responsibilities of adulthood.

Nowhere is the dependence of middle-class girls more animated than in relation to financial needs. Brookes and Kelly observe that right from tweenage, young people submerged in consumer-media culture are at home with how identity and "a sense of self can be fashioned from the resources to be found in the market place" (2009, p. 602). This is the reality of middle-class Kenyan girls. Middle-classness is rooted in financial wherewithal, and performing middle-class girlhood requires financial resources. Therefore, as a financial subject, the middle-class girl coming-of-age is a dependent "independent." Financial dependence limits independence claimed by and about middle-class Kenyan girls. In the United States as in some other parts of the world, as was the case with indigenous Kenyan communities where young people were expected to be contributing members to communities' day-to-day life, some young people are able to get small jobs to raise pocket money. With Kenya's unemployment rates, and because this is simply not a practice in Kenya, middle-class girls do not typically work to raise money. And yet, the social media driven performance of middle-classness, unlike in past generations, motivates attention-seeking consumerism and encourages nonessential spending. This underscores the need for teenagers to have access to funds because children and young people are participants in the culture of gratuitous consumption (Kehily, 2012, p. 256). Unable to work, teenagers must ask for money from the very people they desire no interference from, resulting in what is essentially a compromised independence, and spoiled girlhood.

While this may be a characteristic of most coming-of-age youths, the Kenyan reality is heightened by the fact that even the most basic of responsibilities expected of teenagers across the world, like keeping one's room clean, or assisting with simple chores are often absent in Kenyan middle-class households because they rely heavily on home service labor providers such as maids, gardeners, handymen, and watchmen (Shiino, n.d., p. 42). The new practice of giving unearned weekly allowances to children among the middle class, the offering of rewards to children for every little effort they make in the home, and the presence of house servants responsible for picking up after the girls and boys leaves little investment in the contribution of children to the functioning of the home. Parents focus more on developing networks and skills that make children competitive among their peers in the public sphere. While this is admirable in what it offers the children outside the home, it does contribute to the breeding of entitlement. It is also contributing to a post-feminist mentality among Kenyan teenagers. As Pomerantz, Raby, and Stefanik (2013) outline, postfeminism endorses the ideas of girls as "independent," and yet acquiescent to the pressures and interests of a global economy. They engage in gratuitous consumption without interrogating the gendered nature of global capitalism (Pomerantz et al., 2013, p. 186). A post-feminist mentality further contributes to a performance of girlhood that nurtures entitlement as girls fail to grasp the need to fight for social and political agency on issues that are still present and urgent for many women. Those who espouse post-feminism, strategically navigate their position of being trapped between sexism and post-feminism (Pomerantz et al., 2013). Others claim the tag "feminist" without actively embodying it.

Entitled girlhood reduces understandings of agency and independence to an absence of interference by adults. Such vanity resistances contest input by others in what they do even as these others continue to finance the girls' lives and middle-class lifestyles. Before coming-of-age, performing self-absorbed girlhood, which enjoys dependency with little responsibility or expectations, draws few questions. Before coming of age, the girls have the luxury of still being "children." Older coming of age girlhood anticipates in most cultures, by its very label—a statement of action—growing into responsibility and a journey toward maturity for the initiate. As they come of age, the unmasking of the limits of presumed independence of middle-class Kenyan girls begins. Their dependency on others, necessary to actuate middle-class girlhood, in comparison to other Kenyan coming-of-agers is glaring. This underlines the limits of agency of a young person who is not perceived as a full citizen, and who subsists at the munificence of others. Thus, while shifting rituals of girls in some ways unsettle the status quo, the extent of girl agency, and whether these rituals support their process of maturing and coming-of-age remains in question.

Using Schechner's definition, their liminal state would mean that, in that phase, they are identityless. This signals a movement into a phase where they then take on new identities, and are "initiated into new powers" (Schechner, 2013, p. 66). In this way, an agency that comes with new knowledge, information, and skills related to the initiates' responsibilities to the community is endowed on them. Indigenous processes of coming of age involved an imparting of powers, but most crucially, knowledge. The initiates, thus, received the instruction of coming-of-age as directly stated or implicitly suggested in day-to-day interactions, and the assignment of responsibilities. To initiate means to accept with formal rites into a group, in this case, into adult society, but it also involves the introduction into some special knowledge—new ways of knowing and being. For Kenyan middle-class coming-of-age girls, the disconnect occurs in the space between the preliminal stage and the emergence of new identities, where the inscription of new knowledge and powers should occur. The work of the liminal stage that would bridge these two stages and result in the birth of new identities and powers is erased. There is no framing of this transition, in dialogue, ceremonies or other rituals, and so they never enter a clearly defined liminal stage. As a result of this absence, there are steps that are skipped in the process of learning maturity and acquiring new identities. With an elimination of the observances of initiation, the process of activating the powers as attached to personal and societal responsibilities, and their application in practice is jettisoned, leaving the resulting "independence" dubious.

The evacuated space in socializing of girlhood by collective adult society suggests that the onus is on girls to selectively adopt rituals from different influences to create their own unique culture. This begs the question of whether this has obliterated collective societal coding of girlhood and left girls as each other's primary peer-parents in processes of coming of age. Is societal coding of coming of age girlhood dead?

Middle-Class Coded Coming of Age

The coding of girlhood in relation to agency and power in cultural subjects can be explored through the study of girl and sisterhood principles, girl politics, expressions of intimacy, inclusion and exclusion from groups, codes of belonging, education types, fashion and beauty, parties and celebrations, forms of entertainment and leisure, the arts—including music, family relationships, and work. The clustering and cliquing culture at this age is rampant precisely because girls have not affirmed individual identities and self-concepts (Wiseman, 2009; Adler and Adler, 1995). This limited understanding of the self impacts the reproduction and standardization of codes of performing gender and class. Having not affirmed self-concepts encourages the very interdependence necessary for the sustenance of this group culture and feeds the maintenance of an influential non-individualized socialization of performing girlhood. When this is looked at in tandem with the need for parents and girls to invest heavily in the development and sustainability of a distinct middle-class culture to maintain status, it is clear that while religious or indigenous coding of girlhood may be on the decline, in their place, middle-class codes have materialized. These are evolving extremely fast in the age of common physical teen hangouts including malls as well as virtual hangouts like Instagram, Snapchat and Whatsapp groups.

Indigenous and religious codes of girlhood have, hence, simply been replaced by middle-class codes. Coming-of-age for middle-class girls operates under the oversight of middle-class social institutions, which demand codes of identification and operation to belong. Girls, representing a middle class that is bent on defining exclusivity adhere to coding not just as age peers, but as part of families, polities, religious institutions, and educational institutions, all economically and socially constructed to locate them as middle class. Coding the middle class is an ongoing process and does not start in teenage, nor does it stop there. Such general middle-class coding, therefore, cannot mark unique transitions and expectations related to coming-of-age or performing girlhood. Yet, to be maintained, middle-class belonging has to be constantly earned, and the very need to meet those elite codes allows for new forms of regulation. While teenage codes may appear to operate independently and offer privacy and autonomy to the youth, middle-class codes, in fact, inform a middle-class coded teenage, creating new opportunities for regulated girlhood and young womanhood. Indeed, coming-of-age girls represent one of the age groups that most visually code class on their bodies through accessorizing, makeup, as well as language and physical body performances. The need to wear the right brand, be the right size, carry the right electronics, belong to the right clique, use the right lingo, be invited to the right parties, date the right boy, socialize with the right group of friends, or socialize in the right places, is ever present. Herring and Kapidzic (2015) articulate the fact that the motivation behind self-presentation is often the need to impress others (p. 1).

This mastery of middle-class codes is embraced and handed down by older girls and women. To understand this middle-class coding as unique from other demographics, consider the new phenomenon with the slogan "forty is the new twenty." This supposedly empowering philosophy can also be shaming to forty year olds who do not present as younger, beautiful, or with "it." Meant to be self-affirming in relation to the beauty and strength of maturing women, an analytical lens needs to be directed at the question of where and to whom can forty be the new twenty? Can forty be the new twenty for a lower class or lower middle-class manual labor working body? Or, for the coming of age girls, if forty is the new twenty, then what is fifteen? The latter question invites debate on whether the practice of mothers identifying as younger affects the teenage girls as the gap in age between the two is symbolically reduced.

What separates middle-class coming-of-age in Kenya from others is its unique elitist coding, and the fact that an individual's coding of the self must make room for their identity as middle class. It is a girlhood that panders to marketing machines of goods and services. Coding the self for middle-class girls further involves cultural rewritings and relocations, traversing global cultures to initiate a girlhood that is functional in the Kenyan space as well as global spaces either virtually in the digital world or in physical interactions. A marriage of middle-class coding, universal trending coolness, and dependence on others, therefore, constructs the performance of coming-of-age girlhood in this demographic. The middle-class real and virtual worlds collude in determining patterns of interaction, belonging and exclusion, controlled to a large extent by expenditure. Therefore, performing the kind of girlhood demanded by ways of middle-class being, while it may appear to bestow on girls, as a collective, influence in the society, also forces the self-erasure of individual girls' voices and characters.

CONCLUSION

Proper understanding of girls' identity constructions, as Willis (2009) argues, requires a true engagement with agency, considered in relation to larger societal discourses of femininity (p. 97). Reading girl cultures, codes, and language through the filter of personal agency allows for a profound appreciation for the relationship between the larger society and emerging constructions of girlhood. Kenyan middle-class girls' exercises in self-segregation and the resultant birth of a collective intersubjectivity in the techno-development domains as well as in direct social interaction is not immune to adult and societal influence. Therefore, their performances of girlhoods are constituted as a bundle of conflicting commitments, contesting the larger society and yet requiring the generosity and approval of that very society. While coming-of-age rituals and celebrations may have been lost, the regulation of girl bodies and behaviors is maintained through new class specific codes, adherence to which is ensured by the girls' dependence on their communities, and the need to claim their belongingness within *ubabi* culture. Ever present social media makes more efficient the processes of institutionalizing and moderating these girlhoods.

NOTE

1. A definition has been offered in the introduction.

THREE
The Production of Bridehood

Montemurro's observation in *Something Old, Something Bold: Bridal Showers and Bachelorette Parties* that rituals of women's status transition have been understudied (2006, p. 71) is particularly valid today in relation to contemporary spaces across the African continent. Another scholar, Lisa Walker (2000), intimated that the bride was not enough of a sexy topic, calling attention to the "anxiety that the bride produces for feminist critics" (p. 219). She saw this anxiety as presenting in the stark lack of attention in theory to bridal identities and spaces. As feminist critiques of weddings decrease, opportunities open up for re-reading and reevaluating bridehood and weddings beyond the binary valuations of empowering versus disempowering. Studying women's contextualized experiences with weddings and wedding planning delivers nuance to what Blakely describes as "dichotomous discussions of liberation and domination, romanticism and disenchantment" (2008, p. 22). Because, as Leeds-Hurwitz (2002) states, weddings happen deliberately and by design, they provide a valuable site for studies on and the understanding of personal and collective choices and trends (p. 9).

In Kenya, contemporary bridehood, a brief and impermanent state, appears to have as its single object, logistical preparation for the wedding. It would, therefore, be easy to read brides simply as bodies participating in a series of patriarchal rituals leading to a traditionally patriarchal institution. In this chapter, I argue that, in the construction of modern day bridehood among Kenya's middle class, this seemingly inconsequential state is reconstituting courting and wedding identities. It is precisely bridehood's flexibility, impermanence, and, sometimes, redundancy that makes it powerful as a site for mutinous womanhood that can radically redraft gendered societal scripts.

As rituals of womanhood and girlhood go, today, weddings more than any other state deliver a change in an individual's relationship status (Besel, Zimmerman, Fruhauf, Pepin and Banning, 2009, p. 98). The bride's unique location as an identity marking transition between patriarchally defined unattached freedom and bound wifehood imbues it with great potential for rebellion, as much as it does with capacity to perform compliant womanhood. The wedding is no longer a ritual assumed to mark the changeover from youthful freedom to adulthood (Otnes and Pleck, 2003, p. 5), and more mature brides are likely to make more considered ritual choices. The election to settle down later reworks the very setting of bridehood, and is one obvious way patriarchal womanhood is challenged. As more middle-class women opt to settle down at an older age, their more informed and measured choices of bridal rituals help to create wedding cultures, which influence other women, even those marrying younger.

The facility to instigate change that saturates bridehood begins with the fact that while weddings are important and complex events (Leeds-Hurwitz, 2002; Montemurro, 2006), most of the ritual parts connected to the larger event[1] (Schechner, 2013) happen during the pre-wedding period where one performs most of their bridehood. In Kenya, pre-wedding events include indigenous community rituals, European and American borrowed, as well as church based actions. Imbued with such broad cultural pluralism, bridehood delivers one of the most complex hybridizing conditions and processes in the journey through girlhood and womanhood. The pursuit of Americanization and Europeanization by Kenya's middle class has ensured that the same colonial and religious ideologies that drained women's public power (Odhiambo, 2007, p. 651; Muhonja, 2010; Oduol and Kabira, 1995) have destabilized portions of indigenous bridal practices. One outcome of colonial and Christian interventions was the transformation of marriage into a religious institution, and for Christians, this centered European and American bridal practices, many patriarchally grounded.

Besel et al. elaborate on European and American style wedding rituals, "that the man is the initiator and the woman is the responder. By simply looking at the beginning of the wedding process, it is clear that men and women begin on unequal ground" (2009, p. 101). This statement typifies relationship practices of post-colonial middle-class Kenyan communities and informs on where brides have been located in this history. Still, Kenyan brides, like most brides, need, and middle-class brides now have the social and economic capacity, to personalize the cultural memory and rituals they encounter. Bridal practices offer different abstractions to patriarchy, and the deliberate personalization of bridal rituals frames brides as responding to and restructuring a fundamentally patriarchal process.

The received view that bridal agency is compromised by the collective ownership of bridal identities and spaces (Lieu, 2013; Nash, 2013) is rooted in some historical and pragmatic truths. Coontz (2006) elucidates that for many societies, marriage was, until the late eighteenth century, too important as an institution economically and politically, for its design to be left up to just the couple. This was particularly important considering couples could "base their decision on something as unreasoning and transitory as love" (Coontz, 2006, p. 5). While the role of marriage has significantly evolved, many societies are still collectively invested in marriage as sacred, and the desired state for every adult citizen. Judgment is still directed at women who do not honor this collective appropriation of bridehood and bridal bodies by circumventing traditional bridal activities through eloping, entering cohabitation arrangements, or opting out of marriage entirely. Bridehood, therefore, demonstrates both societal expectations and women's responses to those expectations.

Across cultures, including Kenyan ones, brides have historically understood the moral order attached to the transition into wifehood (Montemurro, 2006, p. 13). Christian cultures in Kenya, even more than indigenous ones, proffer strict societal edicts of bridal performance (Mbunga, 2010). They situate Christian bridehood as a pastiche of the church's bridehood to Christ. Warui, an evangelical minister, quotes Ephesians 5:21–24[2] to back this claim. His explanation that a woman is a bride from the moment the family and the church offer their support of the engagement (Warui, personal communication, June 21, 2014), suggests that her acquiescence to a proposal is inadequate to assure bridehood. The support of her church requires her already always-submissive state to be worthy of bridehood and wifehood. Another minister in Kitale City, Pastor Njue[3] explains that, "A young woman must prove herself as worthy of being a wife. Men don't just propose to anyone" (Njue, personal communication, June 20, 2014). Shibboleths of modern Christianity, which domesticate women through parochial location of female bodies, characterize normative girlhood, early womanhood, and bridehood in relation to preparation for wifehood.

Linking the wedding process and ceremony to marriage as a sacred institution contributes to weddings' attractiveness (Otnes and Pleck, 2003, p. 5), and also means that the morphing of a woman into a bride traditionally involves a series of puritanizing rituals. This construction of apropos bridehood culminates in the apogee ritualistic representation marked by the whiteness of the wedding gown. It is this image, which Lisa Walker describes as "implanted at the level of deep psychological structure, and its appeal cuts across boundaries of age, size, race, sex, and sexuality," (2000, p. 222) that most represents, symbolically the idea of the bride today. For the Kenyan bride, this formulation of bridehood is accompanied by heavy borrowing from diverse cultures, and this delivers to bridehood the freedom to exercise inventiveness. Brides' individual investments in the identity "bride" scripts new identity performances through processes engaged in three sections of this chapter, namely, erasure of patriarchal meanings, decentering of patriarchal influences, and the creation of new meanings and centers of influence.

ERASURES OF MEANINGS

Across cultures, the wedding is symbolic and provides information on the participants' status as members of a community. Howard presents etiquette and taste as forms of power, which allow one group to define acceptable ways of being in a community and coerce the following of others (Howard, 2008, p. 23). This assessment demonstrates the extra appeal of weddings for the middle class, and the allure of weddings has prompted performances, which informed the claim by Wall Street analysts that the wedding industry is recession proof (Ingraham, 2008, p. 38). While lavish weddings are not necessary for the transition into wifehood and husbandhood (Otnes and Pleck, 2003, p. 5), for the middle class, few events exhibit publicly, especially to their immediate circle, their claim to high social standing (Pauli, 2013, p. 154). Extravagant weddings are one of the most powerful ways, which are accessible to all, to advance social approval (Otnes and Pleck, 2003, p. 5; Olanga, Gesage, and Murungi, 2015; Olanga, 2015). As Howard explains, taste has always been used to express or judge social identity or class status (2008, p. 23). This truth, a strong motivator in Kenya, decenters the sacred and a lot of the practical reasons behind the crafting of middle-class weddings, and begins the process of erasure of meanings.

Berardo and Vera (1981) report on the traditions of institutionalized arrangements progressively or precipitously mutating, and causing adjustments to heterosexual relationships (p. 395). As the bridge between wifehood and singlehood, the bridal identity is constructed against an(other). Many indigenous Kenyan communities historically honored woman-to-woman marriages (Njambi and O'Brien, 2002; Oboler, 1980, 1985), but in today's middle-class Kenya, where, legally, bridehood is a female expression of heterosexual relationship commitment, this "other" is masculine.[4] This commitment is expressed through a series of religious, legal and cultural contractual rituals that pre-affirm the end contract, the marriage certificate. These sub-contracts and rituals attached to weddings are acutely rooted in culture, making it hard for weddings to not propagate some patriarchal values (Besel et al., 2009, p. 102).

Performing in this cosmos riddled with contradictions and tensions, bridal choices of Kenyans could be read as compromised by its construction against a masculine identity, and to a large extent, operating in spaces controlled by powerful patriarchal cultures. However, a keener examination of bridal rituals uncovers distinct originality among brides and a fabrication of a new normal of brideliness is emerging. This section of the chapter investigates this remodeling of itself and traditional institutions by Kenyan bridehood.

Two processes are at play in what at quick observation may appear to be standardized performances of bridehood. First, repetitious mimicry waters down the connotations of traditional bridal rituals and then normalizes the shrunken versions, disenfranchising the practices. Consider the following example. Not one of the forty-eight Kenyan men and women, among those interviewed, who consider a proposal incomplete without the presentation of a ring on bended knee, could articulate a reason beyond the fact that it is romantic. Indeed fourteen responses, from eleven women and three men, were similar, verbatim: "It is not a proposal without a ring"(personal communications, 2014–15). The conveyance and embedding of rituals to new cultures is easily sustained when, as Leeds-Hurwitz explains, every wedding propagates the same symbols and practices, and so people forget that humans construct rituals (2002, p. 94). Yet, because, as Ingraham reveals, many modern day ring practices are lies and recent constructs (2002, p. 78–86), it is not surprising that significance of the ritual is so easily neutralized, and among Kenyans, the proposal with a ring presents as just a performance of affective "sophistication."

The second process occurring is the personalization of bridal practices, allowing brides to contrive not just rituals, but their meanings and importance. In this way, brides center themselves and how they want to be perceived, and accordingly encrypt the rituals with new intentions. A bride's inability, in the past, to revise or regulate wedding rituals was advised by the weight and import entrusted to marriage in societal organizing and management, and rituals were necessary to protect the institution. Coontz (2006) expounds on her earlier point:

> For centuries, marriage did much of the work that markets and governments do today. It organized the production and distribution of goods and people. It set up political, economic, and military alliances. It coordinated the division of labor by gender and age. It orchestrated people's personal rights and obligations in everything from sexual relations to the inheritance of property. Most societies had very specific rules about how people should arrange their marriages to accomplish these tasks. (p. 9)

A diminishing of the purpose and functions that Coontz (2006) expresses in contemporary societies allows brides, in the selection of rituals leading up to marriage, to conceive new bridal comportments. In Kenya, the borrowed and revamped practices still present mostly as copies of European and American practices, but the modes of adoption and application result in new relational and sex-performance dynamics and values. Consider as an example the implications of the refashioning of the bridal shower on celebrations of womanhood, as well as how the adoption of gift registries are interacting in entirely different ways with value systems in Kenya than they might in the United States.

The bridal shower, an invention meant to solicit support for the wedding and the outfitting of the matrimonial home (Montemurro, 2006; Leeds-Hurwitz, 2002; Otnes and Pleck, 2003; Ingraham, 2008; Engstrom, 2012), is made irrelevant by two factors in contemporary Kenya. First is the practice of establishing gift registries at various department and service stores,[5] and second is that most middle-class Kenyan brides already have functional homes of their own and do not need to stock a home from scratch. Instead of doing away with the event, Kenyans have imagined a new purpose for it, now redesigned to defy patriarchal traces by degendering it, and also designing showers as settings for free expression of female voices and sexuality.[6] Often, bridal shower gifts are directed toward the bride's comfort sexually or otherwise, and not for the household.

The erasure of values of the bridal shower event, its staging, and the significance of gifts geared toward domesticated wifehood extends to the wedding ceremony. The emergence of a strong gift registry industry is affecting indigenous wedding gifting practices. Gift registries substitute the gift presentation sessions at weddings, deleting key rituals of indigenous culture weddings. This cleanses the gifting rituals of the lessons that would typically accompany the delivery of culturally symbolic gifts to the bride, which extended community control over the position and role of the bride in her matrimonial home.[7] Among the Gikuyu, Luhya, Luo, Kalenjin, and Akamba,[8] the gifts presented, while they might have had different value and meaning in indigenous societies, today, with the heavy gendering of societal organization, could be read simply as supporting the domestication of women. Expunging this ritual scraps the attached patriarchal messages, most of which have been rewritten over history to benefit men, and which, when delivered at weddings as indigenous wisdom, are often accompanied by quotes from the bible.

While much of the erasure of meaning of indigenous Kenyan wedding rituals happens through non-practice, the erasure of meanings in foreign and Christian rituals is most achieved through repeated practice. Spronk's (2009) observations on the performance of a middle class identity for young Nairobians demonstrates this aptly. This demographic, who consider themselves "modern the African way" (Spronk, 2009, p. 511), are unenthusiastic about indigenous ways of being, but also reject "Westernization" and hold onto Africanness as central to their identity (Sponk, 2009, p. 510). Embracing European and American wedding rituals, for the middle class, is matched with significant rejection of attached patriarchal meanings of the rituals. In effect, what they have embraced the most, brides also compromise its meanings. The following quotes from brides demonstrate the process of negotiating meanings as they discard the practice of the groom not seeing the bride in the wedding dress before the wedding, a practice with deep sexist roots.[9] Anita states, "I don't see the sense in it. It is convenient for my boyfriend and I to be together that night. Plus our wedding is an evening wedding. Am I supposed to stay out of my house all night and then all day? I'll not be going anywhere" (personal communication, June 22, 2015). Because the hotel where their wedding was held offered them two nights stay free, Migale and her groom stayed the night before the wedding and the night of the wedding. She explains, "We had already reserved our honeymoon flights out for the day after the wedding. So it made sense to stay the two nights we did" (personal communication, June 13, 2016). Grace explains her situation: "We already have a kid. We live together. I am not a bashful bride. Why would either of us be uprooting ourselves to find somewhere to go when we have a perfectly beautiful house in Kilimani?" (personal communication, July 13, 2014).

The same negotiation is happening with wedding photography as renowned wedding photographer Abraham Ali explains (personal communication, June 24, 2015). Traditionally, as borrowed from European and American practices, wedding parties in Kenya have taken pictures in the time between the wedding ceremony and the wedding reception. More and more wedding parties stage wedding photo shoots before the wedding day. While this new practice is driven mostly by a need for organizational, time, and cost efficiency, and, in the age of social media, the desire to have better pictures staged leisurely, it also represents a deliberate choice by the brides that contests a patriarchal practice (Ali, personal communication, June 24, 2015).

For this research, I watched endless hours of Youtube wedding videos posted by Kenyans, and Kenyan bridal and wedding TV shows, which reveal, among wedding parties, the same lack of privileging of meanings of borrowed rituals as that exhibited by the brides and wives who participated in this research. Even some service providers, in what is now a very lucrative wedding industry in Kenya (Olanga et al., 2015; Olanga 2015) do not understand the origins of some of the services they offer. For both brides and service providers, the interest is in creating perfection and participating in middle-classness. According to Engstrom (2012, p. 122; pp. 149–150), popular media benefits from and contributes to the pre-occupation with the creation of a perfect bride. A proliferation of wedding reality TV shows and bridal expos in Kenya is indicative of not just the growth in the industry, but also bridal quest for perfection. The major TV networks in Kenya produce their own wedding shows: *The Wedding Show* on Citizen TV; *My Dream Wedding* on Kenya Television Network sponsored by *Samantha's Bridal Magazine*; and *Ndoa* on Nation TV. Various American wedding shows also air on cable TV channels available in Kenya and on some Kenyan television networks. These shows include *Say Yes to the Dress, Brides of Beverly Hills, My Fat Gypsy Wedding,* and *Whose Wedding Is It Anyway?*

All the newlyweds and brides interviewed for this chapter who had access to the necessary TV channels confirmed religiously watching Kenyan and American wedding shows especially *Say Yes to the Dress* and *90 Days to Wed*, reading American bridal magazines, and frequenting websites such as *The Knot* as resources for their wedding planning. Ten of the twenty-eight brides and wives who responded to the question on the source of their wedding dress, indicated having bought their wedding dresses from the United States. Three more had made their orders from friends and family in the United States at the time of their interviews. With all these resources for planning, as well as options for service providers, the middle class Kenyan bride occurs like the "superbride"[10] described by Blakely (2008, p. 21). It is to this "character" that the wedding planners and vendors market their goods and services, and not to the community. Understanding this allows for an appreciation of brides as holding the power to reorder the entire industry, and so the society's construction and management of wedding processes.

Besel et al., on wedding production, observe that if people buy into the idea of the wedding day being the most important day of their lives, it is easy to be convinced of the need to invest huge amounts of time, money, and energy (2009, p. 118). The focus in middle class Kenyan weddings is on producing the perfect spectacle. All but five of the brides and wives participating in the research for this chapter indicated the need to have their wedding as close to their vision of perfection as possible. Most of them, however, admitted to the substance of the rituals, if present at all, being secondary to exhibitionism, which Montemurro observes is a part of most portions of wedding celebrations (2006, p. 151–157). In this middle class reality in Kenya, even religious and indigenous cultural exercises, for some, become simply empty duties to fulfill — items on a checklist. Weddings, in this way, become a place where local ritual practices are melded with middle-class consumption habits of Europe and America (Pauli, 2013, p. 153). These changes in consumption related to wedding production are connected to the building of social class (Pauli, 2013, p. 153), and the audience of peers and families (Leeds-Hurwitz, 2002, p. 94) in this over-the-top orchestrated pageantry, in Kenya, are mostly fellow middle class members. Thus, the gendered norms and expectations that would govern wedding ritual selection and performance are no longer the central instigator. Instead, performance of class is.

This erasure of meanings and patriarchal texts from rituals is explained easily by another fact. In considering cultural globalization, for a culture or cultural practice to turn global, it must, in some ways, departicularize and shed of some of its original values to appeal to a wide range of people across the globe. The rituals of middle class Kenyan bridehood, therefore, while still representing perfect heterosexual exhibitionism, are also not very much inspired by patriarchal exactitude that comes with practices being contained within one culture. And so, the Kenyan middle class bride and her party mostly perform to a gallery of social peers. The wedding pageant is complete with costumes, props, music, cues, rehearsals—even a director—the wedding planner, with the bride as the executive producer, the entire process recorded visually and audio-visually for Youtube, and other social media sharing. Lights, camera, action! The result are wedding productions, one more elaborate than the last, in a display of what Kristin Blakely refers to as, "the commercialization of intimate life" (2008, p. 10). In this way, the trend of staging a perfect public spectacle, a perfect look for herself and her party assisted by beauticians and wedding day look fixers, a perfect ceremony, décor, cake, and bridal bouquet, along with the perfect "something old, something new, something borrowed, something blue"[11]—is passed on. New erasures of meaning generate deviations of influence as brides add their own twist with each (re)production.

DECENTERING PATRIARCHAL INFLUENCE

Bridehood is a cultural and social condition and entity, and not biological. It is therefore not necessary for the actualization of womanhood. Ingraham reflects that people are not born as brides or even desiring to be brides (2008, p. 4). This fact liberates bridal identities in a space like Kenya's inter-ethnic middle class, as they find opportunities to confront patriarchy without worrying about conceding some notion of acceptable Luo, Gikuyu, American, Nandi, European, or other womanhood. Operating under the influence of three major patriarchal mega-cultural spaces, in fact, releases the bride from having to commit fully to one or the other in selecting wedding rituals. Accordingly, the betrothal and wedding processes among Kenya's middle class are a potpourri of cross-cultural and intercultural rituals downgrading the influence of American and European culture, Christianity, and indigenous Kenyan cultures. For example, for many couples, bridal acceptance of the engagement ring preempts the outcome of what then amounts to staged community deliberations of practices like *kumenya mucii*[12] among the Gikuyu, *khuselela/kuselela*[13] among the Luhya, and *ayie*[14] among the Luo. The ceremonies become hollow performances feigning permission granting for a marriage that is already assured. Indeed, the presence of the engagement ring on the bride's finger at these events is the loudest statement on the redundancy of the formalities. Among the Gikuyu today, for example, the *nguracio*, customary wedding, can even be held after the legal union takes place.

Mair correctly points out that there are very few generalizable practices and principles of African customary marriages, and it is impossible to reach any credible findings in research that generalizes observations (2013, p. viii). One aspect that allows for generalization, however, is the role of the family. I will now examine that, using the case of the Gikuyu, to illustrate this fading influence of different cultures the bride operates within. Families in pre-colonial indigenous cultures were a central part of the courting and betrothal processes of young people (Kenyatta, 1978; *Uhiki*). Peter Kiarie explains the non-private nature of marriage among the Gikuyu people, calling it a public matter (*Uhiki*). The betrothal ritual, where the groom or his family and friends visit the bride's home, is often the only indigenous practice included in pre-wedding processes of some middle class members today. Indigenous wedding practices ensured that the groom and his people were answerable to a community for how they treated the woman upon marriage. The fact that the laws of Kenya supersede indigenous cultural sanctioning systems means that most middle class brides deem their rights secure under the law (Otieno, 2014; Marriage Act 2014). In fact, this security in part feeds the disregard for indigenous cultural betrothal and marriage practices. Thirty out of thirty-three brides and wives who responded to the question on family involvement were certain that they would choose or would have chosen to get married without the blessings of the family or church if they were confident in their choice of partner. To the question, "When did your bridehood begin?" all but eight shared variations of the same answer: "After we got engaged and announced our engagement"; "After my engagement" (personal communications, February 2014—November 2016). Many women, while respecting their families, treat the family participation in this process as a courtesy. Realizing their lack of legal and social power, it has become more difficult for families to stand in the way of a proposal once the bride assents.

This attrition of time and worth allotted to indigenous rituals is further evidenced by the habit of contracting into fewer meetings what used to be a process comprising a series of visits between the families. Among the Gikuyu, *kuhanda ithigi, kumenya mucii, ruracio,* and *ngurario*[15] may be combined into one or two visits. This, while providing time and financial convenience, indicates a diminishing regard for these practices. Abby explains, "I honestly had no idea what was going on. I just showed up" (personal communication, June 14, 2016). Angela shares that she, too, like many brides, just showed up and did what she was asked to do. She did not invest in researching the events. The only part that concerned her was making sure that she and her groom had purchased everything her mother told them was necessary, and that their parents had enough money to throw an impressive party (personal communication, June 27, 2015). The collaboration of most brides and grooms in sourcing gifts and funds, which the groom is supposed to offer the bride's family, is itself telling.

By cooperating in funding the visit, the couples make two statements, the first being that they are draining the practice of its purpose. The second is that the outcome of the visit is inconsequential to them and has no sway on whether or not their union will take place.

A dilution of that which various visits to homesteads would offer by way of information on any one family that potential in-laws would be seeking occurs. The protracted betrothal process presented opportunities for the two families to establish stronger ties with each other, and also to action investigations into the ways of life, bloodlines, and characters of the families they were about to get into a relationship with. The modern bride's inattention to the rituals and practices' details locates her as primary, often the only custodian of any extensive knowledge about the potential in-laws, which her family would need to offer an opinion on the union. Her community, therefore, has little information upon which to base contestations of her choice. Further, with the two families denied an opportunity to bond through these visits, familial expectations, and oversight over the wedding and marriage are radically eliminated. This state of affairs is supported by the geographic separation and the loss of authority of extended families, and a spotlighting of the nuclear family in societal organizing among the middle class. With this social and physical disconnection of families, selective invitation of whom to involve in the wedding process is possible, ensuring control by the bride's inner circle of the extended community's function and influence in the wedding and marriage to follow.

Following the indigenous betrothal ceremony, many couples participate in the Christian ritual of posting banns.[16] This tradition offers the opportunity for the expression of ideological or legal challenge or hindrance to the union. Like the family visits, the unbinding nature of this practice locates more power and agency in the hands of the couple. The banns for hire arrangement common in Kenya, where couples pay to post banns at churches they have never attended, and where nobody knows them defeats the purpose of the banns. Similarly, the hiring of wedding ceremony celebrants releases brides and grooms from necessary alignments with the churches' positions, requirements, and rituals including pre-wedding counseling.[17] Brides can therefore reduce the church's influence in the planning of the wedding ceremony, and by so doing ease the church's sway on the marriage.

With power primarily located in the bride and groom, they characteristically proceed with wedding plans on their own timetable that is unencumbered by the calendars of the community betrothal and wedding events. Long before the visit to the families and reading of the banns, some brides and grooms often undertake the ritual of formulating what is commonly referred to as a wedding committee, a handpicked group selected to help the couple with the planning and execution of pre-wedding and wedding activities. It is, in fact, often, the committee that plans the community and church betrothal events. For the committee, these indigenous and religious rituals become just part of events in preparation for the wedding they are already planning. The *ngurario* is thus reconceptualized as not a wedding but one of a series of events that lead up to the wedding. Even practices within the *ngurario* event, like *gutinia kiandie*,[18] are reimagined. As Kiriro explains, "Nowadays it's common to see the bride eat meat in front of the father. In Gikuyu culture it was improper for the bride to eat meat in the presence of the father. In Gikuyu culture, she cannot give the groom a piece of meat in front of her father. *Kiande* is not a cake that the bride should give the groom a piece" (*Uhiki*). The layered messages attached to *gutinia kiandie* are, thus, disregarded or refigured. Philosopher and gender studies scholar Betty Wambui explains that the elder-generation interact with these rewritings with cautious enthusiasm because *uhiki,* the marriage, is still on the agenda, and these ceremonies, however constituted, allow for family involvement. They understand the pressure of modernity as reshaping these practices and, just like the younger generations, are adapting (Kiriro, personal communication, January 3, 2017).

This relocation of power to the bride and groom principally favors the bride. One of the borrowed European and American philosophies of weddings is that it is the bride's day and privatization of the wedding, which in indigenous communities was a communal event, turns it into the bride's event. The wedding committee exists for the express purpose of advancing the bride's (and a little bit of the groom's) vision, philosophies, and world sense, and is made up of people of like mind who are peers of the bride and groom. Wedding committees have usurped the role of the family and larger society as advisors and sponsors on the journey toward the wedding and marriage.

Generational differences in the world senses on womanhood and bridehood surface as mothers and aunts, who historically have had significant roles to play in European and American, Christian, and indigenous weddings, are relegated to observers of the wedding planning process, and guests at their bride's wedding. Indeed, for many weddings set in Nairobi and other cities, parents living upcountry arrive just days before the wedding, sometimes on the day of the wedding, and are informed of their role in the wedding, even told what they will wear like the mother of the bride's dress. Njoki's mother lives in Limuru, which is about twenty-one miles away from Nairobi. She and other relatives arrived for the event on the morning of the wedding (personal communication, June 19, 2016). Buyanzi's parents arrived from their home in Kitale, about 250 miles from Nairobi, two days before the wedding. Her mother shares, "All I did was take pictures with her while she dressed and then my friends and I sang and danced to celebrate her when there was space [in the program]. I also was given five minutes at the wedding reception to speak. Her father also" (Hellen, personal communication, June 30, 2014).

Illustrated in the statement of Hellen, Buyanzi's mother, is the fact that arrogated, too, is the assured role of mothers, aunts, and grandmothers, as the leaders of the celebration. Leading the celebrations through song, chants, and dance in indigenous communities offered the opportunity for mothers to send messages to both the bride and groom about performing married life. Hiring a wedding band has become a staple of middle class Kenyan wedding culture. Juma Odembo, director of Kayamba Africa,[19] the leading and most coveted wedding band in the country shares that the band plays at an average of fifty weddings a year (online communication, July 31, 2016). Wedding band culture disrupts the construction of "proper" traditional bridehood and wifehood in a number of ways. Most notably, their mandate is to entertain and not serve an advisory purpose. This abates the application of song and dance as tools for directing bridal and wifely behavior. In fact, one of primary responsibilities of wedding bands is to get the bride and guests dancing unreservedly, dissenting against the idea of the modestly behaved bride.

The bands typically use songs and dances from different indigenous and popular cultures. Odembo shares, off the top of his head, a not exhaustive list of the cultures whose music his band performs: Luhya, Gikuyu, Kamba, Luo, American, Pokomo, Kisii, Kalenjin, Hindi, Giriama, Samburu, Maasai, Chinese, Meru, Pokot, and Taita (Online communication, July 31, 2016). The fusion of music from different cultures erases the advancing of culture specific lessons. The bride and groom, who select the band and confirm the playlist, have the principal influence on the entertainment and any lessons that result. In all the ways explored in the preceding, bridal practices are fundamentally, transforming betrothal and wedding rituals occasioning transference of influence, decentering patriarchal prescriptions and elder advisors, and centering brides. This opens up opportunities to establish new meanings and centers of influence.

CREATING NEW MEANINGS AND CENTERS OF INFLUENCE

Across cultures, traditionally "appropriate" bridehood prescribes certain presentations visually and behaviorally especially on the wedding day. The modern-day bride is commonly imagined visually in the white dress tradition that started with the 1840 wedding of Queen Victoria (Ingraham, 2008, p. 59). Bridal fashion and the performance of the text of the bridal gown have always anticipated modified, often hyper-feminized, behavior. Among middle class Kenyans, the bridal persona's embrace of the white dress was part of a larger "aspiration" for performances of whiteness conceptualized in various ways. Consider the following song, one of the most popular in celebrating Maragoli brideliness.

Ure, Ure Ure, Ure, Ure Ure
Omwana wa mama, tembea kizungu

Translates to:

Ure, Ure Ure, Ure, Ure Ure (chant)
Mother's child (bride), walk (perform) like a white person

The song is either not indigenous or it has undergone revisions, clear in the Swahili words *tembea kizungu*, and also in the reference to *"uzungu,"* whiteness.[20] It evidently, in this version, postdates the advent of missionary work and colonialism in East Africa, and is laced with colonial ideology that envisions whites as superior to Africans. The song, a part of the Maragoli practice of bridal signifying, conveys the message that performing like a white person somehow makes her more deserving of celebration and even marriage. The whiteness of the wedding gown of the bride walking *kizungu* further solidifies the perceived connection between whiteness and purity, as well as whiteness, desirability, and power. Correspondingly, in walking in whiteness, figuratively and in actuality visually, the bride has successfully arrived at the altar of puritanical excellence and is deserving of the groom, a wedding, and public adulation.

Bridal behavior in today's middle class Kenya is often forthright. The bride, in many indigenous Kenyan and European cultures was expected to tone down her personality and strike a curious balance between sadness for leaving her family, and smiling through grateful politeness for being accepted into the new family. Among the Maragoli of Western Kenya, that curious performance was referred to as *kugoha*, now conflated with and inflated by *kutembea kizungu*. However, even the mothers today, while they implore her to *tembea kizungu*, can no longer expect or assume that a middle class Maragoli bride will execute some version of reserved womanhood.

An agential Kenyan bride is emerging from the hybridity of wedding practices. What the bride traditionally commits to publicly before witnesses in the wedding day covenantal and contractual rituals are often patriarchally defined roles, responsibilities, and life and relationship standards, clear, for example, in the religious pre-marital counseling rooted in biblical teachings.[21] While weddings and marriages existed before the nation-state and penal code, the legal contract is the most binding in present-day Kenya. Weddings in most cultures globally are ceremonies that were born at a time when the state/community and the primary religious entity were bonded. Today's weddings in Kenya show a clear distinction between the religious and legal entities and their associations. An eloping couple, or one that opts for a simple ritual through the Registrar of Marriages without the Christian wedding ceremony, does not have to make the public declarations of devotion and submission that a Christian bride does.[22] For both marriages, only one contract is almost unimpeachably legally binding—that reached with the signing of paperwork provided by the Office of the Registrar of Marriages. Without the marriage certificate, the wedding is just a grand costume party.

The customary wedding has even less influence without the registration. On June 9, 2017, Kenya's attorney general, Githu Muigai, through a *Gazette* notice, indicated August 1, 2017, as the deadline for registering any existing unregistered customary marriages with the Office of the Registrar of Marriage in order to legalize them. Failure to do so would nullify the marriages. The *Gazette* notice further stated that following the August 1 date, parties desiring customary marriages would have to first obtain authorization from the Office of the Registrar of Marriages, where they would receive marriage certificates (Muigai 2017, p. 2671). The wedding and supplementary processes, thus, being simply public performances of unbinding rituals, without the marriage certificate, allow for reduction in rigidity, opening the door to bridal resourcefulness, which recasts new meanings and centers of influence. Below, I investigate this through an exploration of wedding day rituals popular among Kenya's middle class.

The walk down the aisle has become, for Kenyan brides, a location for revolutionary choices and voices, disrupting indigenous, foreign-borrowed and religious scripts laden with patriarchal notions. One such convention is the pervasive imagining of brides in the white dress whose history and politics Engstrom discusses (2012, pp. 133–135). A rising number of brides are undermining the whiteness of the wedding dress with embellishments and accessories of multi-colored African beads, African print fabric swatches, and other elaborations, or borrowing from West African practice by wearing African print dresses. One bride, Wandia, sported a blue demin wedding dress with African fabric accents. Leading photographer, Ali, explains, "More and more brides are deciding on the dress style and accessories in ever increasing African inspired or straight out of Africa made pieces" (personal communication, July 31, 2016). A leading graphics design specialist[23] at *Samantha's Bridal*, the leading bridal magazine in Kenya, who has worked with many wedding images, explains that the visibility of brides choosing to Africanize their bridal fashion and other aspects of the wedding can be traced back to around the year 2000. This trend, he says, continues to draw more participants year after year, and he projects even more creativity going forward, spurred by designers like Monica Kanari of Occasions and Days fashion house (personal interview, April 24, 2017). This inscription of Africanness distracts from the narrative of virginity and chastity while re-centering indigenous cultural images literally and figuratively, modeling strong womanhood.

Decked out in wedding finery, the bride must now "be presented" or self present to the groom. The choice by some brides to forego framing this presentation with Wagner's "Bridal Chorus"[24] challenges European and American world bridal behavior projected onto the music. The Bridal Chorus, like the white wedding dress, comes with prescribed behavior for not just the bride, but also the wedding guests who are cued by the first strands of the music to stand and smilingly receive the bride. New music introduces a bride-defined characterization of the space and the bride. The wedding guests, sometimes not aware what the music will be, have no time to fashion an expectation of the bride's performance, or their own, to the music. The element of surprise and excitement prevents the processing of a way of presenting by the guests.

Literally marching to their own tune, many middle class brides are, in a number of ways, pushing the de-gendering of wedding aisle traditions. Most brides now elect to have both parents walk them down the aisle. This recenters the mother's voice that was a key part of the wedding ceremony in most indigenous Kenyan communities. Of a total thirty-two women who responded to this particular inquiry, twenty-six had or plan to have both parents walk them down the aisle. The remaining six have one or both parents missing. Many wedding parties additionally choose to have the groom similarly walked down the aisle by both parents, diminishing, though not completely erasing, the nuances of "the transfer of ownership" (Chesser, 1980, p. 206) of women's bodies. Walking the groom down the aisle mirrors the giving away of the bride, decreasing the imagery and connotations of one individual being walked down and handed over to another because both make the symbolic journey.

Groomsmen traditionally, in the European and American practice adopted by Kenyans, stand at the altar with the groom while the bridesmaids walk up to them. The bridesmaids and groomsmen, in this arrangement, serve as intensifiers to the figurative bridal walk for presentation to the groom. In recent years, in Kenya, in often intricately choreographed movements, like bridesmaids, groomsmen walk down the aisle. Like the change in music, this rewrites the meanings attached to the bridal walk. Like the reintroduction of the mother's voice at the ceremony, the groommen reproduce the indigenous practice among the Luhya, Luo, Gikuyu, Kalenjin, Kamba, and other communities, where the groomsmen would escort the bride and her maids to the ceremony.

The change in meaning and centers of influence is heightened by transformations in the spaces this walk down the aisle leads. An escalation in numbers of "away from church" wedding locations and the introduction of a plethora of spiritual, not necessarily religious, acts from different cultures refashions the concept, altar. The need by brides to have unique and outstanding decorations ensures the purging of reproductions of the traditional religious altar, with unique altar alternatives in the forms of open spaces, canopies, stages, floral ceremonial frames, pavilions, tents, rainbows, marquees, arbors, trellis, and gazebos. The addition to the altar of non-religious elements and rituals including unity items like sand, or milk, and time capsules, further strips the space of religious subtexts. This is critical because the idea of the sacrifice attached to the traditional altar is telling in relation to bridal and wife identities. The sacrificing of oneself at the altar to become someone completely different, someone's wife, complete, in European and American practices adapted to the Kenyan space, with name change, is imagined differently when the walk is not to your groom at an altar laden with religious nuances.

Arrival at the "altar" and the exchange of wedding rings demonstrates another contestation of traditional practices. Many brides in Kenya, as across the globe, now choose to use personalized vows, or edit the church vows, declining to use church defined wedding vows that demand the devotion, honor, and obedience of one spouse to another. If vows represent the public declaration of spousal commitment and how spouses expect to perform in the new relationship (Currie, 1993, p. 404), the choice to forego patriarchal vows is an act of personal resistance made public. The bride publicly revises, with witnesses, the nature of marital contracts, interaction, and roles.

The sacrifice of the self at the altar, the dramatized "first kiss" that seals the vows of loyalty and obedience, and the unveiling of the bride (Chesser, 1980, p. 207) are exercises that signify the end of purity as one is freed to engage sexually with her new husband. Some Kenyan brides now shun the veil at weddings not as a political statement but primarily for aesthetic value, and convenience. Kenyan brides are replacing veils with alternatives like Maasai and other African head beads and crowns, fascinators, headbands, flowers, and tiaras. Choosing not to cover their faces as a performance of purity, and denying the groom the chance to "unveil" them, brides publicly claim ownership of their bodies and sexuality. In so doing, they present themselves for marriage boldly and on their own terms of beauty and "proper" womahood.

Through performances and choices described in this chapter, the bride is able to maintain the feeling of a ceremonial space, acquire the European quality and Americanity, and middle class belonging she desires, while not assuming the ideological baggage of the patriarchal rituals. The bride achieves pomp and ceremony by borrowing without privileging meanings of traditional wedding rituals from all three influencing cultures. This production, while not completely erasing patriarchal markings on wedding practices, shifts control and influence of rituals and within ritual spaces.

CONCLUSION

This semiotic exploration of rituals practiced by middle class Kenyan brides reveals a compromising of the very substance of various patriarchally constructed practices. As mentioned earlier in the chapter, the received view on Kenya's middle class, mostly urbanites, is that the American and European lifestyles provide the benchmark for proper and popular bridehood, and so brides aspire to the European and American indices of defining appropriate brideliness. While this reading of Kenyan bridehood as seemingly assimilationist is not inaccurate, stopping at that thought with no further analysis results in a failure to capture the fact that the ways in which the cultural borrowing is enacted locates the bridal identity as a site for contravening traditions that limit women's independence, and seek to control their bodies and identities. The emerging bridal identities, in some ways, still conform to patriarchal principles, precisely because marriage and Kenyan religious and secular spaces within which they operate are patriarchal. Nonetheless, through selectively deploying rituals, they are birthing a hybrid socio-cultural condition with new contrivances of power, leaving the brides the most powerful figures in betrothal and wedding processes.

NOTES

1. This considers Richard Schechner's definition of the larger event in the book *Performance Studies: An Introduction* (2013, p. 244–245).

2. The passage states: "Therefore, just as the church is subject to Christ, so let the wives be to their own husbands in every thing" (NKJV).

3. The two ministers requested anonymity, and so their names have been changed to accommodate that.

4. The Marriage Act of 2014 describes a marriage as, "the voluntary union of a man and a woman whether in a monogamous or polygamous union and registered in accordance with [this] Act" (Sec 3(1)).

5. See the website for *Wedding Services Kenya*, as an example of a place one can find an extensive directory of companies and individuals providing wedding related services and goods (http://www.weddingserviceskenya.com).

6. Vendors like Famu Bridal Showers, Lamead Woman Network Trust, and Rare Bliss Events advertise different packages and services on their websites ranging from biblical retreats to exotic male dancers.

7. Cooking and other domestic and household implements were gifted among the Luhya, Gikuyu, Luo, Kalenjin, Akamba, and other Kenyan communities. Also presented in some cultures, like the Gikuyu, were/are bedroom furnishings, where the bride and groom were/are expected to symbolically lie on the bed at the gifting ceremony.

8. For example, gifts at Gikuyu weddings include(d) a bed and bedroom accessories, kitchen gear, and baskets.

9. Hardly romantic and rooted in sexist plotting, it is a relic superstition from a time when many weddings were arranged in the West. The groom was prevented from seeing the bride before the wedding lest he found her unattractive and changed his mind. See "The Surprising Truths Behind Common Wedding Superstitions," BridalGuide. (n.p.), 2015.

10. Referencing brides in the United States, Kristin Blakely describes the superbride as, "part *bridezilla*—an extremely picky and uptight bride who has left nothing unplanned or unorganized—and part Cinderella—indulging her childhood fantasies, acting spoiled and pampered, and being treated like royalty" (2008, p. 21).

11. From an old English rhyme, "Something Olde, Something New, Something Borrowed, Something Blue, A Sixpence in your Shoe," the ritual of wearing or carrying something new, something blue, something old, and something borrowed, which dates back to the Victorian era had the purpose of bringing good luck for the bride. Respectively, the items are supposed to keep the bride connected to her past and family, the new life and family she is beginning and joining, the luck of an already successfully married wife because this was supposed to be borrowed from one who is successfully married; and blue was for purity.

12. *Kumenya mucii* (getting to know the home) is a gathering that facilitates the official introduction of the two families.

13. *Khuselela* encompasses the processes of betrothal and the wedding ceremony among various Luhya communities.

14. *Ayie* translates to "I agree." At this meeting, commitments of bridewealth and to the union are reached between the two families.

15. Respectively, the four ceremonies serve the functions of the groom and his friends stating their intentions; the introduction of the families, and the blessings of the union being sought from the bride's family; holding bridewealth talks; and performing the customary wedding ceremony.

16. This Christian ritual is intended to serve the same investigative function as the indigenous practices of the visits between the families of the bride and groom. The church seeks to ensure that the contracts to be signed on the wedding day are not fraudulent and can stand, and so the church undertakes the due diligence of posting banns.

17. Some couples fulfill the obligatory counseling stipulation required by some churches and ministers by attending just one counseling session with their officiating minister.

18. "The wedding is marked by "*gutinia kiande.*" *Kiande* is the upper part of the goat's front leg. The right front leg of the goat was roasted. The groom splits it at the joint and gives it to the bride. The groom cuts the piece of roasted meat and gives it to the bride, then gives her the kidneys to share with friends." (Amos Kiriro, *Uhiki*)

19. Members of Kayamba Africa perform and offer MC, hosting, and other services at events besides weddings, and have toured extensively globally.

20. The word "*kizungu*" is an adverb crafted from the word *mzungu*, translating as white person and the adverbial prefix "ki-," which means "in a manner similar to." The statement translates to "like a white person."

21. Christian brides and grooms take their pre-wedding teachings from church leaders erasing a significant amount of the family's role in transmitting cultural and social values attached to marriage.

22. The following is an example of vows taken by brides and grooms. "I, ___, take thee, ___, to be my wedded husband/wife, to have and to hold, from this day forward, for better, for worse, for richer, for poorer, in sickness and in health, to love and to cherish, till death do us part, according to God's holy ordinance; and thereto I pledge thee my faith [or] pledge myself to you." (Protestant vows from *The Knot*)

23. Name withheld at the request of interviewee.

24. Many, including church ministers, do not realize that the popular "Bridal Chorus"/"Wedding March" song, "Here Comes the Bride" is secular, and from the opera Lohengrin, by German composer Richard Wagner from the nineteenth century. The use of the song at weddings started with Princess Victoria's wedding processional in 1858.

FOUR

Wifing Bodies (Re)negotiating Selfhood

Marriage, traditionally conceived across the globe, is a hierarchical institution. The symbolically patri-located wifing body in Kenya today supports a nuclear family delineated primarily by European/American and Christian values and practices, which often traditionally socially designate a male "head of household." This arrangement, if related to anatomy, because we are talking about bodies, locates the wife below the head, the part of the body that is also associated with one's mental capacity, and contains various primary sensory organs including eyes, nose, tongue/mouth, and ears. Per this configuration, the wife and children could be viewed as non-thinking passive parts of the body that is the family doing as instructed or guided by the head. This common erasure of the independent self circumscribes the wife as Mrs. *Some(body)*, expected to become *Mama Some(body)*, mother of *Some(body)*. How she (re)produces and relates to these other bodies represented in this analogy in body parts, upward to the head, her husband, and downward to her children, positions her as a good or bad, successful or unsuccessful wife.

Church(wo)manship,[1] which normalizes gendered inequalities has since missionary school training of girls across Africa at the advent of colonialism (Kanogo, 1993; Gaidzanwa 2003; Thomas, 2000), been the standard for good married womanhood. Indeed, early missionary educators, believing that African women were not well trained in the art of good housewifery, directed girls' education in missionary schools toward acquiring skills for good wifing (Muhonja, 2010). Mutongi (1999) details this influence of missionary and colonial ideology on characterizing proper womanhood through the colonial administration's promotion of homecraft education for girls (p. 71–72). Because the African middle class during and following colonialism were the supposed conveyers of "civilized" modern living, which was married in many ways to the Christian religion, churchwomanship primed many Kenyan middle class women's performances of their wifehood. Such a wifehood, exemplified in Ruth's fierce loyalty to her in-laws represented by Naomi (Ruth 1:15–16, The New King James Version), heightened the authority of patrilineal and patriarchal values related to marriage.

Patrilineal and patrilocal constitutions of marriage, family, and society buttress patriarchy, and have historically served the personal and political purposes of protecting family propagation, material property, and intellectual property including skills and trades contained within families. Societal structures and processes built around wives are, therefore, designed to maintain this patriarchal status quo. Today, as elaborated in the preceding chapter, most middle class Kenyan wives commit to three different patriarchal contracts, each with set ceremonies and rituals: the indigenous culture contract, legal matrimonial contract, and the religious contract. These contracts signify that being married comes with prescriptions and proscriptions for wifing, accordingly evaluated—formally or informally—by the community (Henrich et al, 2012, p. 659). What, in patriarchal communities is an imbalanced evaluation of married bodies, disproportionately focuses on the wifing body.

The nuclear family marriage is constructed as a tiered institution in relation to authority located in different bodies (Nzegwu, 2012). Oyewumi (2002) describes the nuclear family as "a gendered family par excellence. As a single-family household, it is centered on a subordinated wife, a patriarchal husband, and children" (p. 2). Therefore, the question arises whether or not the amalgamated nature of these three contracts, up from the one contract Kenyan women entered into in indigenous communities, deliver, through the social and political effects of their shared decrees and adjudication, extra layers of subjugation upon the female body and person. The analyses in this chapter interrogate the question of whether this dynamic implies supplementary suppression on the wifing body, and an even severer erasure of the self.

The introduction of European and American secular and religious marital philosophies and practices particularly targeted the condition of wifehood (Kanogo, 2005; Mutongi, 1999). Through renderings of morality and family values, they focalized compulsory wifehood and motherhood. As a result, sanctions for failure at wifehood prevailed, and in parts, still do, whether because wifehood is completely absent or the marriage "fails." Gaitskell (2005) has explained the role of the church in world history in the promotion of marriage, and wifehood, as well as the reinforcement of motherhood as important and essential for womanhood (p. 252). Socialized by such essentialization, women's pursuits of these ideals resulted in a relegation of their other selves outside the wife and the mother to the sidelines (Smith, 2010, p. 2; Mutongi, p. 72), as wives became Mrs. *Some(body)* and/or *Mama Some(body)*.

The survival and proliferation of the European/American and Christian models of marriage across the globe is due, to a large extent, to its framing as a sacred and private institution (Ooms and Wilson, 2004; Fineman, 2001). This claim of sacredness and privacy has also helped preserve sexist distributions of power and control that endure in the modern-day institution. The bulk of this private character of marriage is experienced in the condition of wifehood. Of all the stages of womanhood, wifehood is the most private and sequestered, and yet predominantly, external players and forces outside the wife have, across histories and cultures, constructed it. The space a new wife obtains physically, relationally, and functionally upon transition into a marriage has historically been pre-designed and is umpired by the larger society. In this reality, wifehood is defined by ideological norms and expectations, yet "good" wifehood is constructed functionally, and refereed based on its interactions with other bodies. The wifing body in conventional conceptualizations of marriage performs successfully only as affirmed by other bodies, either by interacting with them "acceptably" when the bodies are relatives, friends, or suitors, or by rejecting other male bodies in exercises of faithfulness to her husband. Control in defining such success is ceded to husbands, extended family, and the larger community.

The charge to defend the privacy entitlements of the marriage weighs heavily on the wife because the other bodies already belong to the family she marries into, and their defense of that privacy is considered guaranteed as a function of their loyalty to the family. The wifing body, as the only one that, upon marriage, in patriarchal and patrilocal societies, experiences dislocation physically and re-identification through renaming either to get married or following divorce, is the one body in the family that loses selfhood and experiences transferences, and so must seek belongingness. Swai (2006) postulates that the construction of identities is fully understood only by considering broader socio-cultural and historical realities of individuals and their interactions with others (p. 385–6). It is the argument of this chapter that wives' bodies, as instruments of identity representation, responding to, and interacting with social, cultural, and political changes posses the capacity to challenge the status quo and occasion revolutionary (im)balances in the existing dynamics of living while married. An examination of how ritualistic processes wives use to execute or respond to the dynamics of contemporary Kenyan families reveals their capacity to trigger the formation of new identities, femininities, and masculinities.

One failure of feminist scholarship is that it has generally tended to reproduce patriarchal paradigms in the ways it studies wives bodies by centering the very phenomena it criticizes (Nzegwu, 1994; Mekgwe, 2008; Oyewumi, 2002). Feminist scholarship on heterosexual wifehood has often made the mistake of focusing too much on resisting the locations of women's bodies, and too little time on assigning and affirming power and value to wifing bodies. This "resisting" trope cannot be applied in a standard way universally because such spaces for women from different cultures deliver(ed) distinct oppressions, rights, and privileges. I proceed from a position that considers the deliberate and systematic domestication of wifing and mothering bodies across Africa from the end of the nineteenth century and through the twentieth century, a historical fact, and a foregone conclusion (Nzegwu, 2012; Amadiume, 1997, 1987; Achebe, 2005; Wambui, 2007; Kolawale, 1997). Additionally, assigning value to domestic labor undertaken by women is a predetermined detail (Buckles, 2008; Hashmi, et al., 2007; Gordon and Whelan-Berry, 2004). These will therefore not be engaged here.

In this chapter I elaborate on how, like the women of indigenous communities addressed in the studies mentioned above, middle class wives in Kenya today are not just balancing public and private worlds, but strategically using their location to accumulate power and control in the home and beyond. Oyewumi (2000) enlightens on the rootedness of this diacritical quality in indigenous African cultural practices when she states that wifehood can be advantageously and tactically used. She decries the fact that European-style definitions of family have compromised this value of African wifehood (p. 1096). I argue here that middle class rituals of wifehood in Kenya possess capacity to counter this erasure. Toward this case, I extrapolate ways in which middle class women in Kenya navigate the roles, duty, and relations attached to the wife identity to dispense new imaginaries of married womanhood. Explored through this lens, twenty-first century middle class Kenyan wifehood presents as a practice in (re)constructing selfhood. By co-opting the very privatization that was used to establish the modern institution of middle class nuclear marriage and wifehood, women destabilize narratives and practices that erase the individual self-ideologically and functionally. In so doing, they redeliver to the identity of wife some of the power that was appropriated away from women in indigenous Kenyan communities with the introduction of Christianity and colonialism.

Because wifehood exists alongside various vulnerable adult states, such reconstructions reframe gendered adult vulnerabilities that negatively affect the facility of women to contest patriarchal wifehood. I define vulnerable adulthood, typically outlined as those stages of life where adults need care from others especially in old age or in illness, in a much broader sense. I conceive it as referencing states that leave an adult without agency, defenseless, or susceptible to emotional, physical, psychological, or economic harm. For the purposes of this chapter, this comprises circumstances that have historically left women vulnerable within or in relation to marriage including the threat of divorce, financial dependence, demands for specific body aesthetics, unaided house and motherwork, and ageing, all creating potential for marginalization and/or abuse in its different forms.

The repositioning of wifing bodies is happening through processes examined in the two subsections of this chapter. First, an ongoing deinstitutionalization of marriage and wifehood is accompanied by an active self-(re)location of wifing bodies and identities. Secondly, such deinstitutionalization prompts a de-gendering of roles in marriage, which triggers the emergence of new familial cultures and new conceptualizations of the wife vis-a-vis the self. These processes appear to be instigating a return, albeit subtly, to indigenous Kenyan communities' characterizations and locations of wifing bodies instilled with autonomy. This analysis corroborates assertions by critical African studies scholars that the lenses applied so far in reading the nuclear family, modeled along "Western" definitions, have restricted scholarship on the identity of wife and the institution of marriage. Such lenses and approaches have been inadequate in exposing cultural nuances that are delivered to cross-culturally adopted phenomena.

UNDOING INSTITUTIONALIZED WIFEHOOD

Wife is an identity entrenched in society's familial cultures in general, and also in a particular family culture, that of her immediate and extended family. If culture influences one's beliefs and behaviors, the fact that institutions are dynamic and transform in response to their environment, means that individuals who are created by the institutions and who then, in transforming, create and transmit forward the new cultures, transfigure identities. Particular to Kenyan families, the shift from primarily kinship-defined families toward a privileging of the nuclear family must necessarily change the performance of identities contained within the family. What has been missed in scholarship on modern Kenyan women is that in neo-local middle class settings, some Kenyan wives deliberately interpret, negotiate, and deploy traditional female social roles to their advantage. Middle class wives capitalize on their mostly urban and independent, self-sufficient existences to define a new wifing ideal, and institution of marriage. They do this by strategically employing the regard for privacy endowed on marriage by nuclear family philosophies to dismantle the patriarchal hierarchy of bodies that persists globally.

The institution of the nuclear family traditionally juxtaposes the virtues of wifehood with the honor of being a husband. Virtuous wifehood has to be judged and acknowledged by others. As elucidated in the introduction chapter, while being a husband as a conclusive identity happens as soon as the wedding officiant says, "I now declare you husband and wife! You may kiss your bride," there is a lack of clarity on when one stops being a bride, as the wife during her first year of marriage is referred to interchangeably as bride or wife. The statement "kiss your bride" not "kiss your wife" is as instructive as the fact that its message suggests one party's ownership of the other. If they kiss each other, the appropriate declaration should be, "You may kiss each other." The newly married woman in the nuclear family then, post-wedding, exists for a period in a space of mixed identity in which she begins the process of erasure of the single-self and the establishment of the wife, privatized to one man or family.

The conversion of identities symbolically enacted through the "giving away" of bodies into wifehood that are then renamed, and the ritual transference of the bride's person and belongings, situate brides' and then wives' bodies as acted upon in an institution that volarizes privacy. As soon as the marriage is declared, a new private world is created. The wife has the task of safeguarding this privacy even as wedding rituals introduce the female body into marriage as vulnerable. This body, disconnected from her extended natal family, and yet having to earn her place in her married home, seeks to belong, and so transforms, with a new name, to take on the identity and expectations of the new role and home. Such is the reality of institutionalizing wifehood. In the reality of middle class Kenya, a multiplicity of cultural influences complicates this physical, identity, and role transition.

Conventional wedding rituals, in preparation for transition and entry into the institution of marriage, pit selfhood against wifehood, in effect erasing selfhood visually and by public declaration. The bride is walked down the aisle and *given away*, she is then docketed by a ring intended to bind two people together with the declaration, "What God has put together, let no man pull asunder!" This loss of choice to separate disadvantages the subordinated body existing in isolation in a new family, learning new cultures and rituals, which she may not even like once she is initiated into them. Per most indigenous Kenyan communities' beliefs, including the Luo and Luhya, a wife was a visitor in her married home. She kept her membership in her natal home, she did not change her name, and could leave without ceremony unless the parties opted to have one, and return to her birth home should she feel dissatisfied. As particularized in chapter 2, among the Luhya she remained *omundu wo luhya*, a member of the clan, in her natal home, and so such a move was always a homecoming. It was the return to her marital home, should she choose to do so, that required a ceremony. This is quite different from European and American style and religion defined marriages, where the ceremony and ritual in the form of a divorce must be sought to leave a marriage, and yet "What God has put together, let no man pull asunder" intends to block departure options.

This loss of selfhood and agency is observable in another declaration at the wedding, "I now present Mr. and Mrs. Some(body)." Following this, the wife enters her marital space symbolically without legs, carried across the threshold. This sexist practice meant to protect the new wife's chastity, originated in medieval Europe, where the groom simulated the kidnapping of the "reluctant" bride by whisking her away from her family (Monger, 2004, p. 268). Further enhancing the death of options, this exercise was supposed to symbolize the unalterable transition into a new world (Mol, 1976, p. 239), the private world of marriage with unique moralistic norms.

Deinstitutionalizing wifehood through a weakening of the customs that create and sustain patriarchal nuclear family organization, by default, shifts bodies and identities within nuclear family marriages. The calculating co-optation of patriarchal ideologies within marriage by middle class Kenyan wives is happening so subtlety that it is going unnoticed. I look, in this section of the chapter, at ways in which this is transpiring. There is in Christian practice as well as European/American cultures, where marriage is defined as a private institution, the need to keep dirty linen out of the public space. This insistence on nuptial privacy, masked as safeguarding the home and family, in actuality shelters masculine fragility. Kenyan wives are repositioning their bodies in relation to autonomy and power by exercising this endowment of sacredness and privacy on marriage to contest interference from outside forces and bodies.

The family presents with outsides and insides, outsiders and insiders, and outside(r) networks and inside(r) networks. The patricolating wife in many African, European, and American societies traditionally joined a new family, sometimes dwelling together, with close physical interaction of bodies related by blood. These bodies in close proximity directly influence each other and collectively guide the orientation of the new wife into the extant family culture. The American wife, for example, upon entering marriage, starts attending events and holidays principally with her husband's family. Rituals for the creation of new relationships force(d) the relocating wifing body to replace her own traditions, practices, even beliefs, with new ones. In this scheme, she enters an already physically, socially, and philosophically defined and sheltered family culture. Patrilocal living delivers expedient adjudicators in the form of her in-laws who sponsor her transformation. In Kenya, such family intervention, often supported by Christian moralizing that formulates marriage as God's ministry (Mate, 2002, p. 556), increases the demands on the wifing body as it is placed under a moral microscope.

The circumstances of early twenty-first century middle class families are the product of effects of the fragmentation of indigenous family structures as a result of urbanization, globalization, and migration (Therborn, 2004; Yankuzo, 2014; Jensen et al., 2011). Families exist in different global and local environments, a fact that underwrites the decentering of extended family influence. This separation of communities geographically also deteriorates the direct influence of the church on families because most middle class Kenyans live in housing estates and neighborhoods away from churches they attend, limiting interaction with their church community to once a week or less. Performance of proper wifehood as sanctioned by the church is thus curtailed. Alice,[2] who attends Sunday service almost every week of the year shares that she tries "to live well every day, every week, every month, every year. But I have to say; it is a relief living across town from my church. Because of the distance, I feel no pressure to belong to [church] cell groups and I can have a life that is not part of the church" (personal communication, June 14, 2016). Sally adds, "I hate feeling watched and judged. So I'm happy to live my family life in Embakasi and drive across town to [Nairobi] Chapel every Sunday. It's also fun. It becomes a Sunday outing for the kids. We try to do something after church" (personal communication, June 15, 2016). Abby, who lives in Westlands, Nairobi, but attends Sunday service at Nairobi Baptist Church on Ngong Road likes the freedom of having a church community and an "away-from-church" community (personal communication, June 7, 2016). Where a rescripting of churchwomanship does not happen, it is clear that the demands of sociality within middle class spaces inspires some wives to simply separate their church and other womanhoods.

This expressed emancipation of wives from Christianity-championed patriarchal performances of womanhood is further supported by the prosperity gospel espoused by many of the neopentecostal churches that middle class Kenyans attend, including those interviewees quoted above. While church bodies might, as a policy, still espouse soft or hard patriarchy, they are cautious about the contradiction of advocating the health and wealth gospel for all (McClendon and Riedl, 2015; Deacon and Lynch, 2013; Mate, 2002), while at the same time propagandizing the need for wives to give up control of their destiny and lives. Geke, a pastor turned life coach, explains that with women making up the highest number of attendants at mega-churches, such preaching, especially for prosperity- or profit-focused church establishments, would alienate the very middle class women (personal communication, June 16, 2014), and their money. Feminist women and men make up a significant part of middle class Christian populations, and as lawyer, Wairimu, who identifies as a born again Christian feminist, shares, "Being women who have worked hard and succeeded in careers and family development, we are the wrong group to preach submission to. You can't tell me I can be a boss everywhere except when I come home" (personal communication, June 13, 2015). Charismatic Catholic Kegehi adds, "Even my husband is a feminist!" (personal communication, June 21, 2015).

This separation of bodies from extended family and church mitigates the imbalance of power, and the emboldening of husbands to perform hard partriachy by the propinquity to families and other extended communities. Additionally, because the need to efficaciously adopt a new family's cultures and values is absent, wives are free from interference.

The judging of the wifing body by extended community based on how it performs in relation to other bodies is thus intercepted. Rael expresses what many of the wives feel about the involvement of extended family in marriages. She states, "Extended family can mess a marriage. How they want things run is not how you both want. If one allows extended family in, it's gonna mess it. They should be kept off. They should just bless the marriage and stay away" (personal communication, February 9, 2017). Naij shares, "I have learnt to keep them at a distance. I have seen many marriages strained and break up as a result of interference from extended family. We engage in family social events and gatherings but, at any point, if they start getting into our business. I call them out. I just disengage and keep off. It has served us well" (personal communication, February 20, 2017). Wielding the fortification of family privacy and sanctity, wives mediate a wifehood that they control, one imbued with agency. This wifehood manifests in practical ways examined in the following paragraphs.

The journey of institutionalized wifing, which prescribes appropriate framings across the globe, has always started with some form of branding. In Kenyan indigenous communities for example, among the Luhya, the bride wore *eshitiri*, the wedding or marriage bangle, and among the Maasai, the wedding collar. These would be the equivalent of wedding rings of European/American practice. Accompanying this visual marking, in European and American traditions, is the change of name. The branding of bodies, an important task in identity establishment, albeit one that exposes the limitations of words and language can embolden but it can also make bodies vulnerable. Renaming as part of the process of creating wives (Boxer and Gritsenko, 2005; Emens, 2007) is a European and American world practice that became a measure of being "modern" and even religious in globalizing Kenya. It especially became a popular tradition of publicly performing middleclassness. The proclamation of the officiant at the wedding, "I now present to you Mr. and Mrs. X" is the common introduction of a newly married couple to the public.

The process of name changing marks a woman's body (Mrs.) as married in a way that it does not for the husband (Mr.), because Mister could be a married man or not. This sexist branding is heightened by the fact that Mrs. is not used in front of her maiden name or often even before hyphenated surnames. Before hyphenated names, most women use the title Ms. With this in mind, the name change contestation for professional and personal reasons being observed among some of Kenya's middle class today defies not just the erasure of wives' natal identities but also allows them to symbolically maintain an identity outside that of a wife who is always representing a marital unit.

The foregoing, in some ways, replicates the definitions, naming, and performances of relationships in indigenous Kenyan communities. While the children belonged to the father's kinship line in many indigenous communities in Kenya, as mentioned earlier in the chapter, the wife remained identified as part of her natal home and a visitor in her married home. The children took on the identity of their father's family but the wife did not. Like it did for women in indigenous Kenyan communities, the affirmation of the woman that is embodied in this act of self-identification assuages certain adult vulnerabilities. As increasingly more people are open to the idea of marriage not being a compulsory part of acceptable female adulthood, the desire for the label "Mrs. Somebody" is declining, as is the fear and stigma of divorce. This licenses audacious wifehoods reinforced by diminishing expectations of wives to serve in marriages as representives of their extended natal families and the existence of legal protection for the rights of wives and their children. Women are increasingly more comfortable initiating, even celebrating, divorce at freedom parties, as can be observed in Nairobi. Christine (personal communication, January 18, 2017) and Mideva (personal communications, May 16, 2015), who did not undergo name changes explain that transitioning back to unattached living and seeking new connections post-divorce was easier without the necessity of the name re-change.

The magnitude of the impact of bold wifehood becomes clear when one considers that among most middle class Kenyans, family cultures are crafted and maintained to a large extent by the wives and mothers. Unlike in many parts of Europe and North America, where the meta-narrative of "family values" still controls public debates on family, and therefore the private attitudes, functions, structures, roles, beliefs, and ideals within families, middle class Kenyan wives are in a position to borrow from local and global cultures to generate the public as well as domestic cultures of their families. The separation from indigenous cultural oversight, and Kenya having not yet got to the place where the government can exercise near absolute influence over the family, concedes more control to individual families in the creation and application of family values. Progressively, the values many wives choose define the middle class nuclear family culture, and the agential self-centering of women in family cultures consequently tests familism as a philosophy.

Familism demands wifely and maternal self-sacrifice in the interest of the family (Edgell and Docka, 2007; Njue et al, 2007). In Kenya, wives, like those of indigenous communities, are tactically using their placement as managers of the home to control the creation of a new type of institution. The claim that what they are doing is for the advancement of family interests, in this case, progression up the middle class ladder, and protection of the sanctity and privacy of the family from external interferences, safeguards against contestation of their choices. They, in effect, utilize familism to combat familism.

Degendering Family Cultures and Roles

An apparent need for scholarship devoted to revisions that steer away from universalized readings of marital roles is glaring when one considers Kenya's middle class. If attention is not directed at this, the application of gendered lenses to role considerations will persist. Freysinger, Shaw, Henderson and Bialeschki (2013) explain that "Gender is relational; that is, it is constructed and reconstructed in relation to and interaction with other individuals within the contexts of society, culture, and history" (p. 4). The deinstitutionalization of wifehood functionally, ideologically, and relationally among Nairobi's middle class members is engineering new practices of wifing bodies, and this, along with the subdual of wife-work and motherwork within nuclear families is altering dynamics of body placement and role expectations, and so adjusting gender role attitudes.

Through patriarchal lenses, married bodies in a nuclear family are assigned roles of (re)production. The heavy lifting in this arrangement is often assigned to women with expectations of motherhood and unaided motherwork. The conflation of woman, mother, and wife, results in estimations that position procreation and lactation as part of the sexual division of labor. By this consideration, gendered marital roles define how labor in society is divided (Oyewumi, 2003, p. 2–3). The production part of those provisions comprises practical, relational, and fiscal responsibilities. In this section of the chapter, I explore ways in which middle class Kenyan women navigate familial (re)production roles and the bearing of that on the placement of female and male bodies in the family and the larger society.

Globally, women are increasingly interrogating and challenging the wifization of their reproductive roles. At the same time, many middle class women with careers defy assertions that their value should be predicated on their performance as good homemakers and good mothers, or even, as underscored in chapter 2, mothers at all. Angela, a business executive with a corporate organization in Nairobi asks, "Do my MBA and all the thirty-plus people who answer to me at work magically disappear when I walk through the door of my house?" (personal communication, August 29, 2014) Reena rejoins, "My daughter is by far the most precious thing to me. But "me" did exist before her, and the "me" that most people know and respect highly in public is not her mother. It's the HR consultant and company director. And accepting that doesn't take anything away from the value of my motherhood" (personal communication, June 17, 2015).

The transition into wifehood, in many cultures, has traditionally been inextricably linked to transition into a reproductive role, mother. Coontz (2006) historicizes this, elucidating that, when the church successfully instituted sanctions on divorce, between the ninth and the thirteenth century, it heightened the need for men to find a wife whose fecundity was assured with their first, and only attempt at marriage, because they would not have a second chance to ensure an heir (p. 124). The sexualization of motherhood as reproductive wifehood contributes to the promotion of making private the condition of wifehood, and also instigates the allocations of "transgressive" wifehoods and motherhoods. The wife and the mother, so linked, obfuscate the woman, the self. Scholars like Sudarkasa (2004), Pala (2015), Nzegwu (2004), and Muhonja (2016), caution that such collapsing of the mother and wife identities not only encumbers understandings of, but also erases the different identities of women.

While motherhood remains valued by most middle class women in Kenya, the available choice to be a full-time mother or not, as well as the easy availability and affordability of maids and nannies, is dislodging mothering and motherwork, and wifehood, as bound states. A consequence is the slow but sure emergence of a very influential near-equal co-parenting culture across sexes. The growth in numbers of lone parents further divorces the identities mother and wife from each other. This new envisioning of reproductive related responsibilities affects production assignments in the home, which I explore in the following paragraphs as physical, relational, and financial labor.

For Kenya's middle class members, who outsource most physical work around the home, parental labor is limited in its anxieties and demands. Production roles present primarily as financial labor, and relational labor particularly emotional parenting as demonstrated by the following responses from some wives in interviews held on June 16, 2016:

> Oh no! Workwise, I can do everything my husband can do. And he can't do anything I can't do. Oh! Except lift heavy stuff. But then we always get other people to do that so it doesn't count. He cannot fix cars or build decks or any of that stuff husbands in America do. So, we are true equals in our abilities. — Njambi

> Well, I have never really seen him do manual labor and I bring in more money. So . . . — Abby

> He can supervise well. That he does very well. But the actual labor? Naaaaaa (No)! He would have no idea where to begin. — Reena

> He acts like he knows what the people we hire do. And I indulge him because it stops them from overcharging us. But my husband has no clue! If those people left, we would just call the next supplier. — Sylvia

> He can't even supervise as well as I can. He gets impatient. — Mama Michael

I learnt that as long as I know how, and in cases where I don't, Google can help, I do it. When it gets a bit technical, I just call a technician.—Naij

The middle class Kenyan husband has little need to be handy or even stronger physically than his wife. With a lifestyle that allows for the hiring of service providers, for most labor in the home, including watchmen for protection, the advantage attached to physical strength that the hunter-gatherer-warrior men had over the women folk is gradually obliterated. This demands a renegotiation of the men's relevance in the home, and the answer to the quandary is readily provided by a succession of circumstances. As nuclear families move farther and farther away from extended family support, and as middle class fathers and mothers seek to affirm their location as "progressive modern" parents, fathers have become more engaged in processes of day-to-day hands-on child-rearing. Within the reality of middle class Kenyan's, such parenting is primarily emotional and relational, and in no way comparable to the labor and time intensive parenting of the middle classes in the United States or parts of Europe. Sunny defines a "modern" father as "one who is fully involved with the children. He takes them to school, helps with homework, goes for school parents meetings, sports, and organizes trips with the children, and hangs out with them. He gives advice where needed" (online communication, February 8, 2017). Judy (personal communication, February 10, 2017) defines her husband as doing more than his half-share of emotional lifting within the family. She explains, "We don't have defined gender roles." Naij shares, "Ideally, he does not wait to be asked to do something but offers to do it. I believe parenting is team-work." Explaining that they share parenting responsibilities right down the middle, she adds that, if necessary, "there are very few thing my husband wouldn't do. He can cook, clean, and do the dishes, and make sure the kids are sorted."

Because the investment in parenting time and effort is minimal in homes with domestic help, the movement of fathers toward an almost equal co-parenting role definition has not received much contestation and is happening unnoticed by many. The rise in popularity of what many call the "modern" father, and the feminist father, who is engaged in the home is easy to track on Facebook and Instagram as proud fathers share their parenting (mis)adventures. This trend is also perceptible in the rise of popular TV shows like *Dads Can Cook* on Kiss TV, as well as events like the annual family food festival, *Real Dads Cook*. *Real Dads Cook* is representative of many father-daughter/son events, outings, and team competitions held in Kenya on Father's Day and through the year at public and private events. The overt and often exaggerated celebration of feminist fathers and lone parenting males, and increase in numbers of those who consider themselves modern-day-minded men who are not bound by traditional role definitions exemplifies societal embrace of a less gendered parenting culture. Family value discourses, which emphasize mothering over fathering and blur wifehood, motherhood, and womanhood, are on the decrease, even on the pulpit at many churches. The de-emphasizing of mother as the primary parenting figure in Kenyan middle class living is reconstituting wife and husband relationships and functions. Only four of the thirty middle class wives interviewed for this chapter self-locate as subordinate to their husbands.

The makeover in production roles is attended by a new reading of space within and outside the home. I note in beginning this spatial exploration that the designation of what is today referred to in feminist scholarship as the "domestic space" as the wife's domain, in indigenous Kenyan cultures, carried different connotations than it did/does in parts of Europe and America. In indigenous Kenyan and other African communities women were not locked out of public domains. They served in every arena and industry including medicine, business, agriculture, military, entertainment, education, and religious institutions, to mention a few (Ocholla-Ayayo, 1976; Mbilinyi, 1978; Presley, 1992; Nzegwu, 1994, 2001, 2006; Adamson, 1967; Coquery-Vidrovitch, 1997; Kolawole, 1997; Amadiume, 1998; Chandler and Wane, 2002; Oyewumi, 2002, 2003). Much of what, and how, they and others performed in these "public domains" was distilled within the "domestic spaces," including the kitchen, making these spaces functionally and ideologically public, weighty centers of power and authority (Muhonja, 2010). An alternative construing needs to be applied to how middle class wives in Kenya are pragmatically and systematically transposing imaginaries of "the domestic" in relation to power in ways that reproduce the conditions of indigenous communities. I undertake a nuanced appraisal below to uncover how some Kenyan wives are employing control over the domestic/home space to magnify their influence within and outside the home.

In the same way that muscle-man responsibilities for Kenyan husbands are on the decline, women have disposed the majority of their "domestic" responsibilities, but without relinquishing the command that came with their position. The majority of middle class wifing bodies are not domesticated bodies, and yet strategically, wives embrace and co-opt to their advantage and influence the responsibility of managing the domestic domain, the home. Replicating indigenous community practices where wives and mothers had other relatives and community members' assistance, many middle class homes are controlled by the woman in a supervisory role, while servants undertake most of the chores, with the rest shared between husbands and wives. Wives enjoy the control of the home without the drudgery and burden that come with it in Europe and the United States. Indeed, the new trend among the middle class is to try and hire, for domestic help, individuals that are capable of managing most household chores and responsibilities including menu planning, shopping, and assisting children with homework. Some families hire tutors for their children to take away the load of assisting children with schoolwork from the parents.

This shrewd way of appropriating the feminization of the domestic space to their advantage is parlayed into assigning themselves the role of regulators of the domestic and public identities and cultures of the family. Twenty-nine of thirty participants who responded either reported having equal say in the management of performances of identities and roles within the family or having more control then the husbands. The control of the home does not come with much labor. For this reason, instead of shunning the responsibility designated to them by society, through European/American and Christian influence, to establish homes for their families, many middle class Kenyan wives appreciate the power housed in the task assignment. Caroline states, "I knew what I wanted for my house and he doesn't stop me" (personal communication, January 30, 2017). Sunny asserts, "I have a say in everything to do with my children and make most decisions to do with them. I like it that way" (online communication, February 8, 2017).

Wives center their taste and preferences to define women-friendly homes and family cultures, and determine circles of inclusion and exclusion for the family. They use this responsibility to reclaim their participation in designing domestic and public social structures, which, as Aidoo advances, colonialism stole from them and assigned to the men (1985, p. 15). In this scenario, wives repurpose and extend their patriarchally assigned domestic role by creating new socialization standards for their families. The new cultures and social structures that emerge for performing middleclassness are rooted in, and expressed in aspirational lifestyles, especially socially, that are not necessarily bound to the home. Socially, middle class families and couples belong to middle class circles. Because middle class Kenyans epitomize ethnic, racial, religious, political, and cultural diversity, the establishment of a family cultures is predominantly influenced by the performance of a middle class identity, and the interviewees of this research assert that women individually, collectively, and in networks serve as the primary architects of that middle class social culture.

The following accounts of different families socializing practices are telling. "My husband has no idea what our plans are from week to week," Muthoni explains. She adds, "But he and the other husbands and fathers show up and they do their part and have a good time, or not. Now I see many of the men hosting with their wives, or sometimes they take the lead to host family events and outings" (Personal communication, December 16, 2015). Twenty-eight of the wives interviewed enjoy this control and explain that although they pick most activities for the families, their husbands are equally engaged in facilitating them. Alice explains, "*Hakuna kazi hapo* (There's nothing to it/it's not really a task).

With social media and other ways of getting information, all I do is come across something I want the family to do, and I call and make reservations. Or my assistant calls and makes reservations" (personal communication, August 21, 2016). She adds, "I don't mind making our plans because I like being the one to decide what we do. I also coordinate with my friends and their families so we do stuff together."

As they sculpt their families' social lives and cultures, many women maintain independent social lives for personal and official reasons away from the family. Rael shares, "I do travel for business often. I have a live-in house help and I leave the husband to run the home. . . . I do check on phone how everything is going on. Sometimes I combine biz [business] trip as go away holiday on my own. I enjoy getting away from the kids" (personal communication, February 9, 2017). Dr. Aluoch explains about his wife, "She has her time away with her friends, both male and female, by the way. Why not? And sometimes she travels for work. Actually she travels a lot for work and then I am mother and father. I travel too." (personal communication, June 22, 2014), Ali reveals, "My wife actually travels out of the country much more than I do. When I travel, it is usually for gigs locally" (personal communication, June 5, 2015). Naij states about her trips abroad that the "hubby pretty much has everything covered and the fact that the kids are all above five years old, that makes everything manageable. I also have a great support system in my house help and niece" (personal communication, February 20, 2017). Purposefully, and buoyed by their financial independence, wives moderate family social circles and exercises. Mama Otieno asserts, "My husband is a good one. He is always there and helps with everything I plan. But you know, if he refuses, I have the money to take the kids. It's not a big deal. But the other fathers will be there. Then he is just left out" (personal communication, August 27, 2016). She laughs as she adds, "Wouldn't want to see himself on Deadbeat Dads."[3]

Redistribution of control over the domestic and public culture of families favors wives and dispenses to them higher influence over family networks and activities, as well as a significant part of family expenditure, reproducing patterns of many indigenous Kenyan communities in precolonial times. This influence, they exercise right from the start in counterpart participation in establishing a residence. Twenty-four of the women in this study report that they had the greatest sway in selecting where their families currently reside, mostly by using the argument of access to amenities for the children and the family to make their case. Mwangi, a real estate agent operating in Nairobi explains that agents know that buyers are really serious when they are with their wives. "If he comes alone, you do the soft sale because he may not be buying but when madame comes, you know they are now serious," he adds (personal communication, January 19, 2017). Some, among them, Sunny, Naij, Reena, Ali, Judy, share that a significant part of the family property is in their names. Augmenting this authority is the fact that wives have security against financial vulnerabilities, particularly those related to divorce (Harari, 2016), based on their personal financial production and contribution, as well as legal protection of marital property ownership, which establishes women not just as co-creators but as co-owners of property and wealth. The Marriage Act of 2014 states that, "Parties to a marriage have equal rights and obligations at the time of the marriage, during the marriage and at the dissolution of the marriage" (p. 37).

The financial production and property jurisdiction of middle class Kenyan wives challenge imaginings of "head of household," initiated during the colonial era, which gendered the phenomena and also erroneously started treating the concepts family and household as synonyms. Adopted from European practices for census and taxing purposes, to be considered the head of household an individual must have provided more than half of the costs to maintain the home. Per this definition, for most middle class families, where spouses contribute near similarly, both incomes being necessary for the maintenance of apropos class lifestyles, the notion of a head is moot. Most wives work outside the home, as was the case in indigenous African families, erasing remnants of notions of gendered breadwinners. In indigenous African communities, compounds consisted of various households. It was thus hard to identify one person as the head of the household in terms of productivity and provision. To calculate contribution to the family, one would have to consider the wife and all the human labor she controlled, whose contribution would outweigh most husbands' contributions. In polygamous families, especially, the wives would be the heads of their individual households. A computation of their contributions plus that of the human labor they controlled collectively would almost certainly outweigh the contributions of one husband.

The idea of a body with gendered parts representing the family, as analogized at the beginning of this chapter, with the man as the head, in middle class Kenyan families is, thus, annihilated. Dolan argues that in many studies, "the absence of analytical space awarded to agency and social identity inhibits a full understanding of intrahousehold relationships" (42). Misconceptions like the ones alluded to by Dolan have contributed to a fallacy that husbands always control family earnings and expenditure in patriarchal societies. Contributing comparably to the household, couples consult on large ticket purchases like the real estate, cars, education for the children, and insurance, among others. The small ticket expenses as well as leisure and socializing activities, in many middle class houses, as earlier noted, remain primarily under the control of wives. This essentially transfers majority purchasing influence and power in the home to wives.

Some Kenyan middle class wives are employing traditional Christian, European/American, and indigenous communities "roles" and domains assigned to women within the nuclear family to inscribe African womanhood on modern day nuclear family wifehood. The disarticulation of marriage as the assumed goal of every adult woman, decrease of stigma on divorce, and the diminishing of opportunities to participate in marriage for middle class women is chipping away at marriage's typicality and conventionality. This empowers middle class women to perform radical wifing.

CONCLUSION: RECALLING THE INDIGENOUS

Like bridehood, wifehood is an identity that is not necessary for the fulfillment of womanhood. This has made it possible for middle class women to personalize wifehood ideologically and practically, prescribing bodies that matter practically and aesthetically, and highlighting the limitations of traditional definitions of wifehood. Through name affirmation, culture creation, and identity deconstruction and reconstruction, these women in effect repossess the wifing body as more than just a wife of someone and mother of another, as they subjectively control the functions and value of that body. The overhaul of how bodies function within a marriage as middle class wives in Kenya juggle multiple options to ensure their individuality and contentment, is bolstering the shifting of matrices of power and reconfiguring personal agency. As the women reorganize their relationship to other bodies, structures, and roles, they conversely change landscapes of adulthood and recompose wifing as the actively strategic condition it was in many indigenous African communities. This facility to use their wifehood strategically activates redefinition of marital and societal roles and attitudes beyond gendered dichotomies, and their self-(re)located bodies demand new relationships with and to their environments within and outside marriage.

NOTES

1. Informed by Bible readings, which include 1 Corinthians 13:4–13; Matthew 19:4–6; 1 John 4:16–19; Song of Solomon 8:6; Genesis 2:18–24; Ruth 1:16–17; Ephesians 5:22–33; Proverbs 18:21; Ecclesiastes 4:9–12; Philippians 4:4–9; Colossians 3:12–19.

2. Some wives in this chapter preferred anonymity and so their names were changed to protect their privacy. They include Alice, Angela, Njambi, Sylvia, Mama Michael, Mama Otieno, Caroline, Anita, and Muthoni.

3. Deadbeat Kenyan Fathers is a public Facebook page where social media users publish narratives that expose and ridicule men who are not supporting their children or are not involved in their lives.

FIVE

New Spaces, New Identities, New Languages

In order to fully appreciate and properly characterize it in scholarship, it is imperative to continually record shifts in any evolving singularity, and the middle class the research for this book encounters is such a phenomenon. Human cultures are dynamic, and by nature, new cultural identities take time to materialize (Hurtado, 1997; Weinreich, 2009; Gosselain, 2000; Tomlinson, 2003). Emerging cultures particularize their character through fast changing adaptations of philosophies, rituals, and other practices (Leidner, 2010; Cowen, 2009; Diouf, 2003). In the globalized twenty-first century, this constitutes a feverishly rapid evolution process of compounding multiple cultural stimuli. I wrap up the inquiries of this book by outlining this quality in the space that is the contemporary Kenyan middle class, and analyze the social and cultural implications of its immediate transfiguring nature and expansion on the place of women and girls in Kenyan society. This examination focuses on transmutations occasioned by the development of new capital urban centers as a result of the devolution of Kenyan government instituted per the 2010 constitution.

With the creation of county governments in Kenya, what has, in modern history, been a class culture created primarily in Nairobi and Mombasa and then transferred to other regions of the country is experiencing decentering. A review of trends, ethnographic narratives, organizational data as well as news reports from what were smaller towns that now serve as capital cities for different counties reveals a re-characterizing and expanding middle class. Deliberating on the social, cultural, and economic ramifications, I analyze this mutating nature of the middle class first as precipitous upsurge in numbers, and then as a refashioning of cultures and identities.

Cities need the middle class to thrive, and the new capital centers of Kenya's counties are invested in creating and expanding their middle-class bases for the benefit of their economies, as well as cultural and social well-being. Resnick (2015) notes the close relationship between middle-class economic drivers and the promotion of social good (p. 6). Other studies demonstrate that middle-class bodies, lifestyles, and consumption cultures make locations appealing as residential, production, and business destinations (Murungi, 2013; McKinsey Global Institute, 2010; Lufumpa, Mubila and Aissa, 2014; Chinganya, Strode, Crawfurd, Moratti, and Schmieding, 2014; Resnick, 2015; Strode, Crawfurd, Dettling and Schmieding, 2015; Kodila-Tedika et al. 2014; Willy, Kimani, and Musiega, 2014; Geissler; Prince, 2013). The new counties are customizing urban development to generate and accommodate an expanding middle class. The following headlines in major newspapers between 2015 and 2016 demonstrate this pandering to the middle class: "Kisumu Bus Tour Takes Middle-class To Dream Homes" (Mkala, 2015); "No Housing for Low-income Earners in Kisumu as Developers Focus on High-end Clients" (Apollo, No Housing, 2014); "Crystal Rivers Project Set to Change the Face of Machakos County" (Africa for Africa, 2015); and "Second Buffalo Mall Set to Be Built in Eldoret as Developers Eye Middle Class" (Gichiri, 2015).

The middle class, thus, is crafting new urbanities, and in fact, actively gentrifying cities as some of the headlines indicate. Apollo reports, "It is notable that there is a shortage of housing for the middle class in nearly all the major towns. The situation is likely to become even more acute in the coming years with devolution, since many people are likely to move to these urban centers" (Apollo, House Hunting, 2014). These processes that are progressively marginalizing the lower classes, and further solidifying middle-class social and economic influence, are likely to continue for a while as evidenced by the multiplicity of new housing developments in Kisumu, Kakamega, Machakos, Eldoret, and Nyeri. Unless these new centers develop a critical mass of upper-class residents, the bulging middle classes remain the critical force in development socially, culturally, and financially. Development of housing fashioned to accommodate this demographic is typically accompanied by the sprouting of high-end establishments including hotels and restaurants, robust business districts, private schools, clubs, and other leisure and recreation spots, and retail venues especially malls (Lumpufa et al., 2015; Chinganya et al., 2015; Willy et al., 2014; Geissler, 2013; Prince, 2013; Murungi, 2013). Between 2011 and 2017, the numbers of malls, for example, in many cities have swelled. Kisumu now boasts several including Tuffom, Mega City, Swan Center, Mega Plaza, Westend, Lake Basin, and Tusky's. Even the small sized Kakamega now has Holden Mall, Mega Mall, and Walias Mall, the last one housing the University of Nairobi facilities. These advances encourage consumption and enhance public performances of middle-classness, as does the attendance of high-end institutions. Private schools, for example, have established satellite campuses across the country to service this expanding middle class. The Braeburn Group of Schools now has campuses in Kisumu, Nanyuki, and Mombasa, and Makini Schools have developed campuses in Kibos and Migosi.

As accentuated in preceding chapters, locating Kenyanness in labor and consumption, particularly in relation to female members of society, reveals new trends in material and service production complemented by ever-changing earning patterns. Increased access to resources and opportunities for participation in public life have made possible the deliberate handpicking and delineation of middle-class rituals in performing motherhoods, bridehoods, wifehoods, and girlhoods. The strengthening of women's and girls' public involvement and influence is augmented by the fact that the facilitation of devolved government is happening alongside two other significant goings-on. First, the number of women graduating from institutions of higher education and joining the public workforce is at its highest in the country's history. Indeed, this has triggered general public anxiety, birthing the discourse of the "boychild left behind."

It is important to dissect this debate to appropriately locate women and girls' public involvement. Properly historicized as part of the development history of gender justice in Kenya, it becomes clear that the current unsupported "boys left behind" discourse is erroneously defining the point of crisis. With girls not having been relocated to the center of systems, while we may accurately speak of boys in crisis, it would be specious to interpret this as the marginalization of boys. Locating the crisis as girls having replaced boys in the center ignores the still urgent ongoing struggles of women and girls, and the enduring insouciance with which policy makers and administrations approach these struggles. What is transpiring is a function of historical disavowals of the need for gender justice in the country, which took from the boys and society as a whole the opportunity to realize gender equity. Highlighting the lack of concrete data pointing to the boy child being left behind, historian and gender studies scholar Godwin Murunga advices paying "attention to the balance of gendered oppression rather than seeking policy redress to a problem that is diversionary in intent" (online communication, February 15, 2017).

Cultural studies and gender studies scholar Dr. Mshai Mwangola problematizes this misdirected anxiety by pointing out the disparities between responses to the current situation and what was observed at the onset of discourses on gender justice in post-independence Kenya. The received view, then, of the general public and those in power was that the fight for gender equity was "women's business." The benefits from such a struggle would accrue, in their imagination, to only women and girls. Men who participated were considered benevolent and kind. Mwangola argues that girls and women catching up does not equate to girls replacing boys. Indeed, located thus within the history of gender justice in the region, she contends that perhaps such arguments, some rooted in masculine anxiety about what they think they are losing, not just in schools but in politics and development, might finally occasion true gender mainstreaming in "all initiatives and discourses, especially on development" (E-mail communication, February 13, 2017). Such mainstreaming, would secure the very rise of influential performances of womanhood and girlhood manifesting in the counties.

A second development happening alongside devolution is, like devolution, assured by the constitution of Kenya, which mandates that one-third of elective and appointive public office holders be from one gender (The Constitution of Kenya, 27 (8)). The consequence of these advances is that going forward, women will make up a significant part of this new expanding middle class, cementing their influence on the creation of political, economic, social, and other cultures across the nation. Kenyan counties are birthing flourishing middle-class environments into which women will not have to fight for later inclusion, as was the case with the early development of cities like Nairobi and Mombasa.

The history of urbanization in Kenya, coupled with the domestication of women's role as a result of colonial and missionary intrusion (Kanogo, 1993; Thomas, 2000; Odhiambo, 2007), masculinized the public elite workspace, and so the formation of the public middle class dispositions in cities during and following independence. Women in colonial Kenya were treated with suspicion and actively discouraged from patronizing cities. Moreover, limited and shared city accommodations for working African men discouraged cohabitation, supporting policies that kept women in the rural areas while their husbands proceeded to cities to work (Odhiambo, 2007, p. 652). This, along with the privileging of education for boys over girls, and the colonial design of school curriculum for the domestication of girls (Kanogo, 1993; Muhonja, 2010; Thomas, 2000) resulted in the sidelining of women in the creation of modern Kenyan cities, and as a consequence, from the formation of early contemporary middle-class culture. Such a history corroborates the significance of the presence and involvement of women and girls in the construction of the new social, cultural, physical, and economic cityscapes in the counties.

The expanding numbers of publicly active female middle-class members, made tenable by devolution and other founts, and their amplified capacity to influence cultures, manifests in a number of ways. The most obvious way is through the rising economic influence of women and girls. We must, first, in considering their power to influence earning and spending cultures acknowledge the unsettling and unclear relationship between women and the capitalist machine that produces the goods and services that sustain the growth of middle-class codes and cultures. Banet-Weiser (2015) acknowledges women and girls' empowerment as "important elements of subjectivity," but cautions that empowerment can also be commoditized (p. 185). It is problematic to speak in absolutes on what the first point of stimulus is between women and the system within which they operate in relation to consumption habits and production patterns. It is also accurate to postulate that a capitalist consumption-driven world, in many ways, encourages and then preys on the vulnerabilities of women and girls. However, examining this relationship through lenses that locate women as empowered consuming citizens who impact culture, social life, and ultimately economies offers an alternative perspective and reading as I offer in the following.

The influence of middle-class women on trends in material, service and business production in expanding cities is undeniable (Willy et al., 2014, p. 86). Middle-class living in Kenya today, mirroring indigenous Kenyan communities, as explored in the chapters of this book, puts more resources and control in the hands of women. At the same time, it demands proper packaging of class status, increasing motivation to spend. In this way, brandishing increasingly the superior purchase power explicated in chapter 4, women sway decisions in processes of designing and planning cities. Certainly, capitalism and globalization have commoditized womanhood and girlhood within Kenya as it has done globally (Lukose, 2005; Pollen, 2013; Willett, 2008; Jatua, 2009; Click, 2009; Black and Sharma, 2001; Ringrose, 2010). Nevertheless, approaching this demographic as the drivers of material and non-material production of goods and services consigns substantial clout to women and girls. Consumerism, a mainstay of middle-class cultures in relation to middle-class Kenyan womanhood and girlhood, influences identity performances as much as identity performances influence consumer production. For the purposes of the arguments of this chapter, no matter which comes first, in so far as the choices, codes, and cultures of women and girls affect the ebb and flow of markets, especially in the creation of new emerging urbanities, such effect must be considered in calculations of control of economic power.

In the case of Kenya, an obvious spike in femvertising (Davidson, 2015; Abitbol and Sternadori, 2016; Rodrigues, 2016), like the Trust condom *Mpango wa Kando*, and *Always Straight As* TV commercials,[1] is indicative of marketing to women's and girls' power. Banet-Weiser, astutely observes that "positioning of girls as 'in crisis' and in need of empowerment and, simultaneously, as important consumers, has helped to create a market for empowerment" (2015, p. 183). She elaborates: "As girls have been increasingly recognized as an important consumer demographic, the power in 'girl power' has become an increasingly malleable concept, lending itself to commodification and marketization" (Banet-Weiser, 2015, p. 183). I concur with her point, but add that we must expand our readings of this relationship. What else is important to consider is the fact that such advertisements, along with online media campaigns, indicate recognition of emerging economically powerful technologized urbanized womanhoods and girlhoods. This dovetailing of girls' and women's cultures, and commodity culture is directing middle-class refinement across Kenya.

Increase in numbers activates the annexing and occupation of more space across the nation by middle-class actors. With devolution, the creation and performance of middle-classness is experiencing transplantation to more places and people across the country. The appeal of migration to Nairobi or Mombasa is eroded by the existence of opportunities, services and goods closer to home in emerging capital cities. The earlier concentration of the contemporary middle class and their cultures around Nairobi and Mombasa was driven in part by the need for people to travel to these cities in pursuit of higher education in an age where there were very few universities serving the entire country. Upon graduation, many stayed to work for establishments in those and a few other larger sized cities like Kisumu and Nakuru (Agesa, 2004; Agesa and Kim, 2001; Macharia, 2003). Consequently, the educated elites were hoarded in these cities. Today, counties are establishing universities and other institutions of higher learning closer to home, as well as new opportunities for businesses and careers better designed for upward mobility. University of Nairobi and Kenyatta University, for example, have established satellite campuses in various counties in the following towns: Embu, Kakamega, Mombasa, Kisumu for the former, and Ruiru, Kitui, Mombasa, Nyeri, Nakuru, and Kericho for the latter. Many more independent private and public universities continue to be established in the counties. This, along with many large companies gradually setting up shop in the smaller cities, persuades regional migrations to cities other than Nairobi or Mombasa.

It is also arguable that these developments have activated a process of de-urbanization. Kenyans staying in their rural homes can access specialized goods or services from cities closer to home. Under these circumstances, some professionals, able to find lucrative jobs in regional cities, are opting to maintain rural homes and commute to work. This trend is observable around Nyeri, Kisumu, Kitale, Kakamega, and Machakos. In Nairobi, with the development of better transport infrastructure, sub-urbanization is a growing trend and more professionals commute to work from rural homes or neighboring towns like Limuru, Kikuyu, Kiserian, and Athi River (Wagikondi, 2013; Njuguna, 2013). The significance of this for the debates of this book is that the urban monopoly on the character of the Kenyan middle class is eroding and a stronger rural middle class is emerging. The rise of regional and rural educated elite populations, the growing appreciation for regional and rural living, and the proliferation of higher education opportunities and jobs promote de-urbanization and regional urban migration. Farmers and other service and goods providers, themselves a budding middle-class set who service these regional and rural elite, augment the increase in numbers of a regional and rural middle-class demographic.

Female members, a significant part of this population, through intra- and inter-socialization in the physical and virtual worlds, perform in local, national, regional, and global milieus. With socializing peers for women and girls changing with concurrent processes of globalization and devolution, the resulting subcultures for the different regions sport unique eccentricities. The character(s) of the women of these new middle-class populations proliferating across the country in different locations will, therefore, be further diversified and such differentiation will be locked in by a number of factors.

First, competition is inherent in middle-class living as exemplified by this demographic's exercising of consumerism (Ansori, 2009; Fernandes, 2008; Gerke, 2000; Kharas and Gertz, 2010; Murungi, 2013). Expressive practices can position bodies and language as locations for articulations of power by conformity or competition. These contests of consumption and lifestyle supremacy are today heightened by the presence of new virtual and digital world platforms for staging and exhibiting middle-classness. Kenyan women and girls perform their rituals selectively in real life, and then share those performances in the same digital worlds that might have instigated the physical world performance in the first place as witnessed in Facebook, Twitter, and Pinterest interactions. This cyclical nature of motivations for middle-class expressions, and the public character and reach of social media, forces self-representations that compete with other womanhoods and girlhoods, locally and globally. This competition is a statement on middle-classness and not sisterhoods or womanhood. Within the middle class, the need to fit in and claim status is directed at peers, mostly other middle class members who share class status first locally and then nationally and globally. The desire for virtual world middle-class affirmation of one's extraordinariness is resulting in the supplementing of conformity to general class codes with particularized garnishing.

This particularization involves localization of middle-class codes, which will generate distinct identities of women and men of the different regions of Kenya. Driscoll convincingly captures the role of environments in the definition of location, identity, and culture specific girlhoods (2008, pp. 22–23). Region specific performances and rituals are in part vanity and pride driven, but may also be determined by environmental factors like weather, physical environment, local cultures, and available resources, which affect specific leisure, fashion, language, lifestyle, and business choices. The surge in beach vacation activity and businesses taking shape around Kisumu City, inspiring a new breed of domestic and international tourists and beach performances of middle-classness in the region exemplifies this. Machakos City on the other hand is primarily marketing itself as a business and sports recreation destination, and a quick weekend and holiday getaway and playground for middle-class members from Machakos, its environs, and Nairobi. Concerts, and other cultural events tailored to the interests of the middle class, recreationally complement these getaways. These examples of factors contributing to the emergence of region-specific middle-class identities and performances are reproduced with contextualized markers across the counties.

These unique pronunciations of girlhood and womanhood can already be unveiled in trends exhibited online and in social media groups like Kisumu Mums, Kisumu Mums marketplace, Kilimani Mums, Kilimani Mums Marketplace, Kisumu Expats, Nairobi Expats Marketplace, Machakos Mums Marketplace, Mombasa Mums Marketplace, Kakamega Mums, Kakamega County Mums, and Kilimani Mums Nyeri branch. Blogs and podcasts, YouTube channels as well as traditional media including regional and vernacular FM radio stations like Lolwe FM, Mulembe FM, Muuga FM, Chamigei FM, Mururi FM, Suswa FM, Mayan FM, Kitwek FM, Mayienga FM, Kaya FM, Anguo FM, Ramogi FM, which Nyabuga and Baker (2013) argue, "target educated, middle-class, urban audiences, hence leaving out rural people," (p. 75) offer more proof of this phenomenon.

Insofar as middle-class progression involves class and other boarder crossings, it also involves boundary erections and this facilitates the nurturing of difference from others, even those of the same class. According to Hassi and Storti (2012), culture defined anthropologically constitutes "an element of identification within a given group of individuals and an element of differentiation vis-à-vis other groups," and sociologically, "artistic and symbolic creations, heritage and cultural products" (p. 6). Applying either conceptualization affirms that group differentiations and unique identity and cultural expressions are inevitably a part of the future of Kenya's middle class. Thus, examining how inscribing regional qualities affects the performance of middle-class girlhood and womanhood is key to the project of understanding the materialization and evolution of the middle class. What, for example, constitutes Kisumu county middle-class womanhood, and in what ways do Kakamega middle-class women's and girls' performances differ from Nairobi's?

Hassi and Storti (2012) extend their argument above, opining that culture is birthed by interactions and within it, individuals fashion societies and communities by delineating norms and relationships and social and cultural codes that mark their uniqueness from other communities and cultures (p. 6). Once rituals are established as common practice in specific regions, locations of conformity, resistance, or transgression often co-mingle with internal tensions and differentials among the diverse people practicing them as they personalize the rituals. The upshot is that middle-class women's identities in Kenya can no longer claim a uniform hybridity, and Nairobi and Mombasa will no longer be the center for the creation of middle class, and consequently, general Kenyan women's and girls' cultures, providing the standard for everyone else to imitate. Through processes of translocal fusion and hybridization, as defined by Hassi and Storti (2012, p.12), unique cultures will emerge and so unique identities. Hybridity as Willis (2009) elucidates, is critical to appreciating how individual, to each girl, constructions of girlhood are, while at the same time being understood as part of the general space of femininity (pp. 102–103). A rich network of middle-class identities and womanhoods swaying, inspiring, and shaping each other are emerging across the country.

Because these new regional capital cities present with distinct ethnic imprints, a likely reality is that these new middle classes developing will privilege more ethnic community-specific markers. The question of whether these region-specific middle-class cultures will begin to reflect more consideration for indigenous cultural traditions, including in relation to girlhoods and womanhoods, then arises. This is a likely outcome considering that historically, for political and other reasons, after colonialism and independence, some Kenyans have refined the art of ethnically othering populations different from their own, even developing languages and names for them, some non-flattering (Ligaga, 2012, p. 10). Some studies indicate that for Kenyans, the ethnic allegiance is in fact often manipulated and deliberately sustained by the elite for political and economic gain (Bratton and Kimenyi, 2008; Bedasso, 2016; Murungi, 2013). Ethnicized middle-classness is therefore a likely consequence of regional middle-classness. The transformations deliberated in this and in preceding chapters will prompt customizations that create diverse Kenyan versions of global middle-class girls' and women's cultures.

CONCLUSION

I started the deliberations of this book with Paechter's (2012) cautioning that "understanding femininities as other to masculinities means that we are always starting with the masculine, and, indeed, the hegemonically masculine: everything then becomes defined in relation to it" (p. 238). I have offered alternative conceptualizations of Kenyan womanhoods and girlhoods that center and locate this demographic as drivers of their own and others' actions and choices. In this reality, contemporary and indigenous culture institutions are forced to face not just the limitations of their definitions of proper girlhoods and womanhoods, but the fact that they are incapable of making such a definition at all. Such patriarchal institutions must therefore let go of the compulsion to attempt characterizations of a standard womanhood and girlhood, as should scholars and classrooms of women's and gender studies. The performances of womanhoods and girlhoods among middle class Kenyans are dislocating traditional religious, European, and American, and indigenous cultures' subjectivities and understandings of femaleness, forcing reconstructions informed by an amalgam of local and global environments, cultures, values and norms. The resulting hybrid identities require new monikers and approaches in scholarship that delineate not just the layered nuances of these new middle-class cultures, but also the power and autonomy now relocated in female members of society.

NOTE

1. The *Mpango wa Kando* TV commercial was a source of great controversy with some lamenting that it endorsed and encouraged infidelity. The commercials can be viewed at https://www.youtube.com/watch?v=lTfpWrG51ms and https://www.youtube.com/watch?v=AWS4lCyPUkc.

References

Abitbol, A. and Sternadori, M. (2016). You Act Like A Girl: An Examination of Consumer Perceptions of Femvertising. *Quarterly Review of Business Disciplines*, 3(2), 117–138.

Achebe, N. (2005). *Farmers, Traders, Warriors, and Kings: Female Power and Authority in Northern Igboland, 1900–1960*. Portsmouth: Heinemann.

Adams, B. N. and Mburugu, E. (1994). Kikuyu Bridewealth and Polygyny Today. *Journal of Comparative Family Studies*, 25(2), 159–166.

Adamson, J. (1967). *The Peoples of Kenya*. New York and London: Harcourt Brace Jovanovich.

Adler, P. A. and Adler P. (1995). Dynamics of Inclusion and Exclusion in Preadolescent Cliques. *Social Psychology Quarterly*, 58(3), 145–162.

Africa for Africa. (2015, October 19). Crystal Rivers Project Set to Change the Face Of Machakos County. *Construction Review Online*. Retrieved from https://constructionreviewonline.com/2015/10/crystal–rivers–project–set–to–change–the–face–of–machakos–county/.

Agesa, R. U. (2004). One Family, Two Households: Rural to Urban Migration in Kenya. *Review of Economics of the Household*, 2(2), 161–178.

Agesa, R. U. and Kim, S. (2001). Rural to Urban Migration as a Household Decision: Evidence from Kenya. *Review of Development Economics*, 5(1), 60–75.

Aidoo, A. A. (1985). Women in the History and Culture of Ghana. *Institute of African Studies: Research Review*, 1(1), 14–51.

Ajzenstadt, M. (2009). Moral Panic and Neo–Liberalism: The Case of Single Mothers on Welfare in Israel. *British Journal of Criminology*, 49(1), 68–87.

Alexander, J. C. (2004). Cultural Pragmatics: Social Performance between Ritual and Strategy. *Sociological Theory*, 22(4), 527–573.

Allen, K. (2015, February 27). The Surprising Truths Behind Common Wedding Superstitions. *BridalGuide*. Retrieved from http://www.bridalguide.com/planning/wedding–ceremony–traditions/wedding–superstitions.

Always Kenya. (2016, August 16). *New Always Ultra*. Retrieved from https://www.youtube.com/watch?v=AWS4lCyPUkc.

Amadiume, I. (1987). *Male Daughters, Female Husbands: Gender and Sex in an African Society*. London: Zed Press.

Amadiume, I. (1997). *Re–inventing Africa: Matriarchy, Religion and Culture*. London: Zed Books.

Amadiume, I. (2005). Theorizing Matriarchy in Africa: Kinship Ideologies and Systems in Africa and Europe. In *African Gender Studies: A Reader* (pp. 83–98). New York: Palgrave Macmillan.

Anderson, D. J., Binder, M. and Krause, K. (2003). The Motherhood Wage Penalty Revisited: Experience, Heterogeneity, Work Effort, and Work–schedule Flexibility. *ILR Review*, 56(2), 273–294.

Aniciete, D. and Soloski, K.L. (2011). The Social Construction of Marriage and A Narrative Approach to Treatment of Intra–Relationship Diversity. *Journal of Feminist Family Therapy*, 23(2), 103–126.

Ansori, M. (2009). Consumerism and the Emergence of a New Middle Class in Globalizing Indonesia. *Explorations*, 9, 87–97.

Anthias, F. (2002). New Hybridities, Old Concepts: The Limits of 'Culture'. *Ethnic and Racial Studies*, 24(4), 619–641.

References

Apollo, S. (2014, January 14). No Housing for Low–Income Earners in Kisumu as Developers Focus on High–End Clients. *Daily Nation*. Retrieved from www.nation.co.ke.

Apollo, S. (2014, January 23). House Hunting Made Easy. *Daily Nation*. Retrieved from www.nation.co.ke.

Argyrou, V. (1996). *Tradition and Modernity in the Mediterranean: The Wedding as Symbolic Struggle (No. 101)*. Cambridge and New York: Cambridge University Press.

Banerjee, A. V. and Duflo, E. (2008). What is Middle Class about the Middle Classes around The World? *The Journal of Economic Perspectives*, 22(2), 3–41A.

Banet–Weiser, S. (2015). 'Confidence You Can Carry!': Girls in Crisis and the Market for Girls' Empowerment Organizations. *Continuum*, 29(2), 182–193.

Barker, V. (2009). Older Adolescents' Motivations for Social Network Site Use: The Influence of Gender, Group Identity, and Collective Self–esteem. *CyberPsychology and Behavior*, 12(2), 209–213.

Baquedano–López, P. (2001). Creating Social Identities through Doctrina Narratives. In E. Duranti (Ed.), *Linguistic Anthropology: A Reader* (343–358). Malden, Massachusetts: Blackwell Groups.

Bedasso, B. E. (2016). For Richer, For Poorer: Why Ethnicity Often Trumps Economic Cleavages in Kenya. *Review of African Political Economy*, 0(0), 1–20.

Bengtson, V. L. (2001). Beyond the Nuclear Family: The Increasing Importance of Multigenerational Bonds. *Journal of Marriage and Family*, 63(1), 1–16.

Berardo, F. M. and Vera, H. (1981). The Groomal Shower: A Variation of the American Bridal Shower. *Family Relations*, 30(3), 395–401.

Besel, A., Zimmerman, T. S., Fruhauf, C. A., Pepin, J. and Banning, J. H. (2009). Here Comes the Bride: An Ethnographic Content Analysis of Bridal Books. *Journal of Feminist Family Therapy*, 21(2), 98–124.

Berry, C., Martin, F. and Yue, A. (2003). *Mobile Cultures: New Media in Queer Asia*. Durham: Duke University Press.

Birdsall, N., Graham, C. and Pettinato, S. (2000). Stuck in Tunnel: Is Globalization Muddling the Middle? (Center on Social and Economic Dynamics Working Paper No. 14). Washington, DC: Brookings Institution.

Black, P. and Sharma, U. (2001). Men are Real, Women are 'Made Up': Beauty Therapy and the Construction of Femininity. *The Sociological Review*, 49(1), 100–116.

Blakely, K. (2008). Busy Brides and the Business of Family Life: The Wedding–planning Industry and the Commodity Frontier. *Journal of Family Issues*, 29(5), 639–662.

Blundell, R., Costa Dias, M., Meghir, C. and Shaw, J. (2016). Female Labor Supply, Human Capital, and Welfare Reform. *Econometrica*, 84(5), 1705–1753.

Boxer, D. and Gritsenko, E. (2005). Women and Surnames across Cultures: Reconstituting Identity in Marriage. *Women and Language*, 28(2), 1–11.

Bradford, T. W. and Sherry, J. F. (2013). Orchestrating Rituals through Retailers: An Examination of Gift Registry. *Journal of Retailing*, 89(2), 158–175.

Bratton, M. and Kimenyi, M. S. (2008). Voting in Kenya: Putting Ethnicity in Perspective. *Journal of Eastern African Studies*, 2(2), 272–289.

Brookes, F. and Kelly, P. (2009). Dolly Girls: Tweenies as Artefacts of Consumption. *Journal of Youth Studies*, 12(6), 599–613.

Brown, J. D., Halpern, C. T. and L'Engle, K. L. (2005). Mass Media as a Sexual Super Peer for Early Maturing Girls. *Journal of Adolescent Health*, 36(5), 420–427.

Buckles, K. (2008). Understanding the Returns to Delayed Childbearing for Working Women. *The American Economic Review*, 98(2), 403–407.

Chandler, D. J. and Wane, N. (2002). Indigenous Gendered Spaces: An Examination of Kenya. *Jenda: A Journal of Culture and African Women Studies*, 2(1), 1–25.

Cheeseman, N. (2014). Does the African Middle Class Defend Democracy? *WIDER Working Paper*, 96, Helsinki: World Institute for Development Economics Research.

Chesser, B. J. (1980). Analysis of Wedding Rituals: An Attempt to Make Weddings More Meaningful. *Family Relations*, 29(2), 204–209.

References

Chinganya, O. J., Strode, M., Crawfurd, L., Moratti, M. and Schmieding, F. (2014). Consumption Patterns. In M. Ncube and C.L. Lumpufa (Eds.). *The Emerging Middle Class in Africa*, (pp. 9–33). New York: Routledge.

Christopher, A. J. (1988). 'Divide and Rule': The Impress of British Separation Policies. *Area*, 20(3), 233–240.

Clark–Flory, T. (2013, October 27). Where Did My Feminist Wedding Go? Retrieved from http://www.salon.com/2013/10/26/where_did_my_feminist_wedding_go/.

Click, M. A. (2009). It's A Good Thing: The Commodification of Femininity, Affluence, and Whiteness in the Martha Stewart Phenomenon (Doctoral dissertation). University of Massachusetts—Amherst, Amherst, Massachusetts.

Constitution of Kenya, The (Revised Edition 2010). The National Council for Law Reporting with the Authority of the Attorney General.

Coontz, S. (2006). *Marriage, A History: How Love Conquered Marriage*. New York: Penguin Books.

Coquery–Vidrovitch, C. (1997). *African Women: A Modern History*. Boulder: Westview Press.

Couldry, N. (2003). *Media Rituals: A Critical Approach*. New York: Routledge.

Cowen, M. (1976). Notes on Capital, Class and Household Production. *Mimeo*. Nairobi: University of Nairobi, Department of Economics.

Cowen, T. (2009). *Creative Destruction: How Globalization is Changing the World's Cultures*. Princeton: Princeton University Press.

Cronk, L. and Dunham, B. (2007). Amounts Spent on Engagement Rings Reflect Aspects of Male and Female Mate Quality. *Human Nature*, 18(4), 329–333.

Currie, D. H. (1993). "Here Comes the Bride": The Making of A "Modern Traditional" Wedding in Western Culture. *Journal of Comparative Family Studies*, 24(3), 403–421.

Davidson, L. (2015, January 12). Femvertising: Advertisers Cash in on #Feminism. *The Telegraph*. Retrieved from www.telegraph.co.uk.

Deacon, G. and Lynch, G. (2013). Allowing Satan In? Moving Toward a Political Economy of Neo–pentecostalism in Kenya. *Journal of Religion in Africa*, 43(2), 108–130.

Dean, M. and Laidler, K. (2013). A New Girl in Town: Exploring Girlhood Identities through Facebook. *First Monday*, 18(2), n.p.

Deardorff, J., Gonzales, N. A., Christopher, F. S., Roosa, M. W. and Millsap, R. E. (2005). Early Puberty and Adolescent Pregnancy: The Influence of Alcohol Use. *Pediatrics*, 116(6), 1451–1456.

Delaney, D. M. (2005). *The New American Wedding: Ritual and Style in a Changing Culture*. New York: Penguin Group.

Department of Tourism, Sports and Culture. Machakos County Government, n.d. Retrieved from http://www.machakosgovernment.com/GovernmentDepartmentsMachakos.aspx?DptID=9.

Dieter, N. and Stoll, F. (2013, June). *One or Many Middle Class(es) in Kenya? Towards an Analytical Frame for Distinguishing Subgroups*. Lecture presented at the European Conference of African Studies, Lisbon.

Dieter, N. and Stoll, F. (2015). Socio–cultural Diversity of the African Middle Class: The Case of Urban Kenya (Bayreuth African Studies Working Paper No. 14). Bayreuth University: Institute of African Studies.

Diouf, M. (2003). Engaging Postcolonial Cultures: African Youth and Public Space. *African Studies Review*, 46(2), 1–12.

Driscoll, C. (2008). Girls Today–Girls, Girl Culture and Girl Studies. *Girlhood Studies*, 1(1), 13–32.

Durham, M. G. (2015). Quvenzhané and the Comedians: Black Girlhood and Sexuality at the "Edge" of Mediated Humor. *Communication, Culture and Critique*, 8(4), 505–521.

Easterly, W. (2000). The Middle Class Consensus and Economic Development (Policy Research Working Paper 2346). Washington, DC: World Bank.

Edgell, P. and Docka, D. (2007). Beyond the Nuclear Family? Familism and Gender Ideology in Diverse Religious Communities. *Sociological Forum*, 22(1), 25–50.

References

Emens, E. F. (2007). Changing Name Changing: Framing Rules and the Future of Marital Names. *The University of Chicago Law Review*, 74 (3), 761–863.

England, P., Bearak, J., Budig, M. J. and Hodges, M. J. (2016). Do Highly Paid, Highly Skilled Women Experience the Largest Motherhood Penalty? *American Sociological Review*, 81(6), 1161–1189.

Engstrom, E. (2012). *The Bride Factory: Mass Media Portrayals of Women and Weddings*. New York: Peter Lang.

Feng, P. C. (2002). Rituals of Rememory: Afro–Caribbean Religions in "Myal" and "It Begins with Tears." *Melus*, 27(1), 149–175.

Fernandes, L. (2000). Restructuring the New Middle Class in Liberalizing India. *Comparative Studies of South Asia, Africa and the Middle East*, 20(1), 88–104.

Fiese, B. H., Hooker, K. A., Kotary, L. and Schwagler, J. (1993). Family Rituals in the Early Stages of Parenthood. *Journal of Marriage and The Family*, 55(3), 633–642.

Fiese, B. H., Tomcho, T. J., Douglas, M., Josephs, K., Poltrock, S. and Baker, T. (2002). A Review of 50 Years of Research on Naturally Occurring Family Routines and Rituals: Cause for Celebration? *Journal of Family Psychology*, 16(4), 381.

Fineman, M.A. (2001). Why Marriage? *Virginia Journal of Social Policy and the Law*, 9(1), 239–272.

Freysinger, V. J., Shaw, S. M., Henderson, K.A. and Bialeschki, M. D. (2013). "Introduction: Constructing A Framework." In V.J. Freysinger, S.M. Shaw, K. A. Henderson, and M. D. Bialeschki (Eds.), *Leisure, Women, and Gender* (pp. 1-20). Alberta: Venture Publishing, Inc.

Gaidzanwa, R. (2003). *Gender and Canon Formation: Women, Men and Literary Art in Africa*. N.p. Retrieved from http://www.codesria.org/IMG/pdf/Gaidzanwa.pdf.

Gaitskell, D. L. (2005). Devout Domesticity?: A Century of African Women's Christianity in South Africa. In A. Cornwall (Eds.), *Readings in Gender in Africa* (pp. 177-187). Bloomington/Indianapolis and Oxford: Indiana University Press and James Currey.

Gakahu, N. and Kaguta, R. J. N. (2011). The Social Implications of A Global Culture to Africa: Kenya's Case. *Journal of Economics and Sustainable Development*, 2(4), 163–170.

Gallagher, S. K. (2003). *Evangelical Identity and Gendered Family Life*. New Brunswick: Rutgers University Press.

Gash, V. (2009). Sacrificing Their Careers for Their Families? An Analysis of the Penalty to Motherhood in Europe. *Social Indicators Research*, 93(3), 569–586.

Geissler, P. W., Kelly, A. H., Manton, J., Prince R. J. and Tousignant, N. (2013). Introduction: Sustaining the Life of the Polis. *Africa*, 83(4), 531–538.

Gerke, S. (2002). Global Lifestyles Under Local Conditions: The New Indonesian Middle Class. In B. H. Chua (Ed.), *Consumption in Asia: Lifestyles and Identities* (pp. 135–158). London and New York: Routledge.

Gez, Y. N. and Droz, Y. (2015). Negotiation and Erosion of Born Again Prestige in Nairobi. *Nova Religio: The Journal of Alternative and Emergent Religions*, 18(3), 18–37.

Gichiri, J. (2015, October 13). Second Buffalo Mall Set to Be Built in Eldoret as Developers Eye Middle Class. *Business Daily*. Retrieved from www.Businessdailyafrica.com.

Gonick, M., Renold, E., Ringrose, J., Weems, L. (2009). Rethinking Agency and Resistance: What Comes after Girl Power? *Girlhood Studies*, 2(2), 1–9.

Gordon, J. R. and Whelan–Berry, K. S. (2004). It Takes Two to Tango: An Empirical Study of Perceived Spousal/Partner Support for Working Women. *Women in Management Review*, 19(5), 260–273.

Gosselain, O. P. (2000). Materializing Identities: An African Perspective. *Journal of Archaeological Method and Theory*, 7(3), 187–217.

Gray, K. R., Shrestha, N. R. and Nkansah, P. (2008). A Cross–cultural Perspective on Management in Kenya. *Journal of African Business*, 9(1), 27–58.

Gregg, P., Harkness, S. and Smith, S. (2009). Welfare Reform and Lone Parents in the UK. *The Economic Journal*, 119(535), F38–F65.

Griffiths, A. M. (1997). *In the Shadow of Marriage: Gender and Justice in an African Community*. Chicago: University of Chicago Press.

References

Gunga, S. O. (2009). The Politics of Widowhood and Re–marriage among the Luo of Kenya. *Thought and Practice*, 1(1), 165–178.

Hall, H. R. and Brown–Thirston, A. (2011). *Understanding Teenage Girls: Culture, Identity and Schooling*. Lanham: Rowman & Littlefield Education.

Harari, M. (2016). Women's Inheritance Rights and Bargaining Power: Evidence from Kenya. Retrieved from https://faculty.wharton.upenn.edu/wp–content/uploads/2016/02/Harari_Inheritance_2016.pdf.

Harris, A. (2004). Introduction. In A. Harris (Ed.), *All about The Girl: Culture, Power, and Identity* (pp. xvii–xxv). New York: Routledge.

Hashmi, H. A., Khurshid, M. and Hassan, I. (2007). Marital Adjustment, Stress and Depression among Working and Non–working Married Women. *Internet Journal of Medical Update*, 2(1), 19–26.

Hassi, A. and Storti, G. (2012). Introduction. In A. Hassi and G. Storti (Eds.), *Globalization and Culture: The Three H Scenarios* (pp. 3–20). INTECH Open Access Publisher.

Hatch, G., Becker, P. and van Zyl, M. (2011). *The Dynamic African Consumer Market: Exploring Growth Opportunities in Sub–Saharan Africa*. Johannesburg: Accenture.

Henrich, J., Boyd, R. and Richerson, P. J. (2012). The Puzzle of Monogamous Marriage. *Philosophical Transactions of the Royal Society Biological Sciences*, 367(1589), 657–669.

Herbst, C. M. (2013). Welfare Reform and the Subjective Well–being of Single Mothers. *Journal of Population Economics*, 26(1), 203–238.

Herring, S. C. and Kapidzic, S. (2015). Teens, Gender, and Self–presentation in Social Media. In J. D. Wright (Ed.), *International Encyclopedia of Social and Behavioral Sciences*. Oxford: Elsevier. Retrieved from http://ella.slis.indiana.edu/~herring/teens.gender.pdf.

Hope, K. R. (2014). Devolved Government and Local Governance in Kenya. *African and Asian Studies*, 13(3), 338–358.

Howard, V. (2008). *Brides, Inc.: American Weddings and the Business of Tradition*. Philadelphia: University of Pennsylvania Press.

Huffaker, D. A. and Calvert, S. L. (2005). Gender, Identity, and Language Use in Teenage Blogs. *Journal of Computer-Mediated Communication*, 10(2), 00–00.

Humphrey, M. (2003). From Victim to Victimhood: Truth Commissions and Trials as Rituals of Political Transition and Individual Healing. *The Australian Journal of Anthropology*, 14(2), 171–187.

Hurtado, A. (1997). Understanding Multiple Group Identities: Inserting Women into Cultural Transformations. *Journal of Social Issues*, 53(2), 299–327.

Hussein, J. W. (2009). A Discursive Representation of Women in Sample Proverbs from Ethiopia, Sudan, and Kenya. *Research in African Literatures*, 40(3), 96–108.

Ingraham, C. (2008). *White Weddings: Romancing Heterosexuality in Popular Culture*. London: Routledge.

Islam, G. and Zyphur, M. J. (2009). Rituals in Organizations a Review and Expansion of Current Theory. *Group and Organization Management*, 34(1), 114–139.

Ivey, D. C. and Conoley, C. W. (1994). Influence of Gender in Family Evaluations: A Comparison of Trained and Untrained Observer Perceptions of Matriarchal and Patriarchal Family Interviews. *Journal of Family Psychology*, 8(3), 336–346.

Izugbara, C. O., Ochako, R. and Izugbara, C. (2011). Gender Scripts and Unwanted Pregnancy among Urban Kenyan Women. *Culture, Health and Sexuality*, 13(9), 1031–1045.

James, J., Ellis, B. J., Schlomer, G. L. and Garber, J. (2012). Sex–specific Pathways to Early Puberty, Sexual Debut, and Sexual Risk Taking: Tests of an Integrated Evolutionary–Developmental Model. *Developmental Psychology*, 48(3), 687.

Jarvis, A. (2007). The Dress Must Be White, and Perfectly Plain and Simple: Confirmation and First Communion Dress, 1850–2000. *Costume*, 41(1), 83–98.

Jatau, M. (2009). Western Media's Commodification and Consumption of African Women: A Review of Three News Channels. *UCLA Center for the Study of Women*. UCLA: UCLA Center for the Study of Women. Retrieved from http://escholarship.org/uc/item/9gs2q469.

Jensen, L. A., Arnett, J. J. and McKenzie, J. (2011). Globalization and Cultural Identity. In S. J. Schwartz, K. Luyckx and V. L. Vignoles (Eds.), *Handbook of Identity Theory and Research* (pp. 285–301). New York: Springer.

Jepkirui, M. M. (2004). Language Planning and Literacy in Kenya: Living with Unresolved Paradoxes. *Current Issues in Language Planning*, 5(1), 34–50.

Johnson, S. B., Blum, R. W. and Giedd, J. N. (2009). Adolescent Maturity and the Brain: The Promise and Pitfalls of Neuroscience Research in Adolescent Health Policy. *Journal of Adolescent Health*, 45(3), 216–221.

Johnson-Hanks, J. (2007). Women on the Market: Marriage, Consumption, and the Internet in Urban Cameroon. *American Ethnologist*, 34(4), 642–658.

Kabaji, E. S. (2009). *The Construction of Gender through the Narrative Process of the African Folktale: A Case Study of the Maragoli Folktale* (Doctoral dissertation). University of South Africa, Pretoria, South Africa.

Kahn, J. R., García-Manglano, J. and Bianchi, S. M. (2014). The Motherhood Penalty at Midlife: Long-Term Effects of Children on Women's Careers. *Journal of Marriage and Family*, 76(1), 56–72.

Kaltiala–Heino, R., Kosunen, E. and Rimpelä, M. (2003). Pubertal Timing, Sexual Behaviour and Self–reported Depression in Middle Adolescence. *Journal of Adolescence*, 26(5), 531–545.

Kanogo, T. (1993). Mission Impact on Women in Colonial Kenya. In F. Bowie, D. Kirkwood and S. Ardener (Eds.), *Women and Missions: Past and Present. Anthropological and Historical Perceptions* (pp. 165–186). Providence, Oxford: Berg Publishers.

Kanogo, T. (2005). *African Womanhood in Colonial Kenya, 1900–1950*. Athens: Ohio University Press.

Karanja, L. (2010). "Homeless" at Home: Linguistic, Cultural, and Identity Hybridity and Third Space Positioning of Kenyan Urban Youth. *Comparative and International Education*, 39(2), 1–19.

Kariuki, W. (2006). "She Is a Woman After All": Patriarchy and Female Educational Leadership in Kenya. *Postamble*, 2(2), 65–74.

Kaplowitz, P. (2011). Update on Precocious Puberty: Girls are Showing Signs of Puberty Earlier, but Most Do Not Require Treatment. *Advances in Pediatrics*, 58(1), 243–258.

Kehily, M. J. (2012). Contextualising the Sexualisation of Girls Debate: Innocence, Experience and Young Female Sexuality. *Gender and Education*, 24(3), 255–268.

Kenyatta, J. (1978). *Facing Mount Kenya: The Traditional Life of the Gikuyu*. Nairobi: East African Educational Publishers.

Kharas, H. (2010). The Emerging Middle Class in Developing Countries (Development Center Working Paper No. 285). Paris: OECD Development Centre.

Kharas, H. and Gertz. G. (2010). The New Global Middle Class: A Cross–over from West to East. *Wolfensohn Center for Development at Brookings*, 1–14. Retrieved from https://www.brookings.edu/wp–content/uploads/2016/06/03_china_middle_class_kharas.pdf.

Kim, Y. Y. (2008). Intercultural Personhood: Globalization and A Way of Being. *International Journal of Intercultural Relations*, 32(4), 359–368.

Kjeldgaard, D. and Askegaard, S. (2006). The Glocalization of Youth Culture: The Global Youth Segment as Structures of Common Difference. *Journal of Consumer Research*, 33(2), 231–247.

Knot, The. (n.d.). Traditional Wedding Vows from Various Religions. Retrieved from https://www.theknot.com/content/traditional–wedding–vows–from–various–religions.

Kodila–Tedika, O., Asongu, S.A. and Kayembe, J.M. (2014). Middle Class in Africa: Determinants and Consequences. *International Economic Journal*, 30(4), 527–549.

Kolawole, E.M. (1997). *Womanism and African Consciousness*. New Jersey: Africa World Press.

Kopelman, R. E., Shea–Van Fossen, R. J., Paraskevas, E., Lawter, L. and Prottas, D. J. (2009). The Bride is Keeping Her Name: A 35–year Retrospective Analysis of Trends

and Correlates. *Social Behavior and Personality: An International Journal*, 37(5), 687–700.
Koster, M. M. (2011). The Kilumi Rain Dance in Modern Kenya. *Journal of Pan African Studies*, 4(6), 171–193.
Koster, M. M. (2016). *The Power of the Oath*. Rochester: Rochester University Press.
Kraidy, M. (2005). *Hybridity, or the Cultural Logic of Globalization*. Philadelphia: Temple University Press.
Kroeker, L. L. (2014). Kenya's Emerging Middle Class(es). *Inequality, Citizenship and the Middle Classes*. Bayreuth Academy of Advanced African Studies, 1–12. Retrieved from https://www.academia.edu/14514641/Kenyas_Emerging_Middle_Class_es_.
Kroger, J. (2004). *Identity in Adolescence: The Balance Between Self and Other*. Oxford: Psychology Press.
Leeds–Hurwitz, W. (2002). *Wedding As Text: Communicating Cultural Identities through Ritual*. Mahwah: Lawrence Erlbaum.
Leidner, D. E. (2010). Globalization, Culture, and Information: Towards Global Knowledge Transparency. *The Journal of Strategic Information Systems*, 19(2), 69–77.
Lenhart, A., Purcell, K., Smith, A. and Zickuhr, K. (2010). Social Media and Mobile Internet Use among Teens and Young Adults. *Millennials*, 1–51. Retrieved from http://www.pewinternet.org/files/old-media/Files/Reports/2010/PIP_Social_Media_and_Young_Adults_Report_Final_with_toplines.pdf.
Lieu, N. T. (2013). Disrupting Nostalgic Scenes of Whiteness: Asian Immigrant Bridal Shops and Racial Visibility in the Ethnoburb. *Spaces and Flows: An International Journal of Urban and Extra Urban Studies*, 3(2), 1–13.
Ligaga, D. (2012). Virtual Expressions: Alternative Online Spaces and the Staging of Kenyan Popular Cultures. *Research in African Literatures*, 43(4), 1–16.
Ligaga, D. (2014). Mapping Emerging Constructions of Good Time Girls in Kenyan Popular Media. *Journal of African Cultural Studies*, 26(3), 249–261.
Little Cake Place, A. (2014, October 28). Keeping the Top Tier—It's a Tradition! *A Little Cake Place*. Retrieved from http://www.alittlecakeplace.com.au/keeping-the-top-tier-its-a-tradition/.
Lufumpa, C. L., Mubila, M. and Aissa, M. S. B. (2014). The Dynamics of the Middle Class in Africa. In M. Ncube and C.L. Lumpufa (Eds.), *The Emerging Middle Class in Africa*, (pp. 9–33). New York: Routledge.
Lukose, R. (2005). Consuming Globalization: Youth and Gender in Kerala, India. *Journal of Social History*, 38(4), 915–935.
Macharia, K. (2003). Migration in Kenya and Its Impact on the Labor Market. *Conference on African Migration in Comparative Perspective, Johannesburg, South Africa*. Retrieved from http://citeseerx.ist.psu.edu/viewdoc/download?doi=10.1.1.596.4329&rep=rep1&type=pdf
Macharia, K. (2012). "How Does a Girl Grow into a Woman?": Girlhood in Ngugi wa Thiong'o's The River Between. *Research in African Literatures*, 43(2), 1–17.
Mair, Lucy P. (2013). *African Marriage and Social Change*. London/New York: Routledge.
Manji, A. (2015). Bulldozers, Homes and Highways: Nairobi and the Right to the City. *Review of African Political Economy*, 42(144), 206–224.
Markson, S. and Fiese, B. H. (2000). Family Rituals as a Protective Factor for Children with Asthma. *Journal of Pediatric Psychology*, 25(7), 471–480.
Markus, H. and Nurius, P. (1986). Possible Selves. *American Psychologist*, 41(9), 954–969.
Martha. (2014, July 4). Personal Communication.
Maseno, L. and Kilonzo, S. M. (2011). Engendering Development: Demystifying Patriarchy and its Effects on Women in Rural Kenya. *International Journal of Sociology and Anthropology*, 3(2), 45–55.
Masquelier, A. (2005). The Scorpion's Sting: Youth, Marriage and the Struggle for Social Maturity in Niger. *Journal of the Royal Anthropological Institute*, 11(1), 59–83.

References

Mate, R. (2002). Wombs as God's Laboratories: Pentecostal Discourses of Femininity in Zimbabwe. *Africa*, 72(4), 549–568.

Mbembe, A. (2008). The New Africans: Between Nativism and Cosmopolitanism. In P. Geschiere, B. Meyer and P. Pels, Peter (Eds.), *Readings in Modernity in Africa* (pp. 107–111). Bloomington: Indiana University Press.

Mbilinyi, M. (1978). Where Do We Come From, Where Are We Now and Where Do We Go From Here? In A. Pala, T. Awori and A. Krystal (Eds.), *The Participation of Women in Kenya Society* (pp.187–200). Nairobi: Kenya Literature Bureau.

Mbiti, J. S. (1990). *African Religion and Philosophy*. Oxford: Heinemann.

Mbunga, J. M. (2010). An Exploratory Study of Marital Satisfaction of Forty Couples at the Africa Inland Church, Jericho, Nairobi, with the View to Inform Premarital Counseling Practices in Kenya (Unpublished doctoral dissertation). Asbury Theological Seminary, Wilmore, Kentucky.

McClendon, G. and Riedl, R. B. (2015). Religion as a Stimulant of Political Participation: Experimental Evidence from Nairobi, Kenya. *The Journal of Politics*, 77(4), 1045–1057.

Mendis, P. (2005). Americanization of Globalization. *Public Manager*, 34(3), 3–8.

Mekgwe, P. (2008). Theorizing African Feminism(s): The Colonial Question. *African Journal of Philosophy*, xx(1–2), 11–22.

Mekgwe, P. (2010). Post Africa(n) Feminism? *Third Text*, 24(2), 189–194.

Milanovic, B. and Yitzhaki, S. (2002). Decomposing World Income Distribution: Does the World Have A Middle Class? *Review of Income and Wealth*, 48(2), 155–178.

Mitchell, C. and Reid–Walsh, J. (2005). CHAPTER ONE: Theorizing Tween Culture Within Girlhood Studies. *Counterpoints*, 245, 1–21.

Mkala, M. (2015, August 13). Kisumu Bus Tour Takes Middle–Class to Dream Homes. *Standard Digital, East African Standard*. Retrieved from www.standardmedia.co.ke.

Mol, H. (1976). *Identity and the Sacred*. New York: The Free Press.

Monger, G. (2004). *Marriage Customs of the World: From Henna to Honeymoons*. Santa Barbara: ABC–CLIO.

Montemurro, B. (2006). *Something Old, Something Bold: Bridal Showers and Bachelorette Parties*. New Brunswick: Rutgers University Press.

Morley, D. and Robins, K. (2002). *Spaces of Identity: Global Media, Electronic Landscapes and Cultural Boundaries*. New York: Routledge.

Mugane, J. (2006). Necrolinguistics: The Linguistically Stranded. In *Selected Proceedings of the 35th Annual Conference on African Linguistics*, 10–21.

Muhonja, B. B. (2008). Notes Towards a Research in African Feminist Theater. *West Africa Review*, 0(12), 45–56.

Muhonja, B. B. (2010). She Loved and Ruled That Kitchen: Space and Autonomy in Kenyan Societies. *JENdA: A Journal of Culture and African Women Studies*, 0(15), 6–25.

Muhonja, B. B. and Owusu–Ansah, D. (2011). Editorial: Africa at the Crossroads. *West Africa Review*, 0(19), 1–5.

Muhonja, B. B. (2014). Race and Social Islands in Kenya's Urban Spaces. In T. Falola and D. Sanchez (Eds.), *African Culture and Global Politics* (pp. 307–323). London: Taylor & Francis/Routledge.

Muhonja, B. B. (2015). Teaching Moments and Negotiating Motherhood. *JENdA: A Journal of Culture and African Women Studies*, 0(23), 33–52.

Muhonja, B. B. (2016a). Gender, Archiving, and Recognition: Naming and Erasing in Nairobi's Cityscape. In M. M. Koster, M. Kithinji and J.P. Rotich (Eds.), *Kenya After 50: Reconfiguring Education, Gender, and Policy* (pp. 171–195). New York: Palgrave Macmillan US.

Muhonja, B. B. (2016b). Mothering at Intersections: Towards Centering Mother Knowledge. In Muhonja B. B. and Bernard W.T. (Eds.), *Mothers and Sons: Centering Mother Knowledge* (pp. 1–21). Ontario: Demeter Press.

Muigai, Githu. Gazette Notice No. 5345—The Marriage Act 2014 (No. 4): Customary Marriage. *The Kenya Gazette*, June 9, 2017, p. 2671.

Munthali, A. C. and Zulu, E. M. (2007). The Timing and Role of Initiation Rites in Preparing Young People for Adolescence and Responsible Sexual and Reproductive Behavior in Malawi: Original Research Article. *African Journal of Reproductive Health*, 11(3), 150–167.

Murungi, C. N. (2013). *The Letter and the Spirit: Politics, Intimacy, and Middle Class Constitution–making in Kenya* (Doctoral dissertation). Stanford University, Stanford, California.

Musandu, P. (2012). Daughters of Odoro: Luo Women and Power Re–Examining Scripted Oral Traditions. *Women's Studies*, 41(5), 536–557.

Mutongi, K. (1999). 'Worries of the Heart': Widowed Mothers, Daughters and Masculinities in Maragoli, Western Kenya, 1940–60. *The Journal of African History*, 40(1), 67–86.

Mutongi, K. (2007). *Worries of the Heart: Widows, Family, and Community in Kenya*. Chicago: University of Chicago Press.

Nash, M. (2013). Brides N'Bumps: A Critical Look at Bridal Pregnancy Identities, Maternity Wedding Dresses, and Post–feminism. *Feminist Media Studies*, 13(4), 593–612.

Ncube, M. and Lufumpa, C. L. (Eds.). (2014). *The Emerging Middle Class in Africa*. New York: Routledge.

Ndlela, N. (2009). African Media Research in the Era of Globalization. *Journal of African Media Studies*, 1(1), 55–68.

Niaje TV. (2013, March 26). *Banned Kenyan Condom Advert*. Retrieved from https://www.youtube.com/watch?v=lTfpWrG51ms.

Njambi, W. N. and O'Brien, W. E. (2000). Revisiting "Woman–woman Marriage": Notes on Gikuyu Women. *NWSA Journal*, 12(1), 1–23.

Njue, J. R. M., Rombo, D. O. and Ngige, L. W. (2007). Family Strengths and Challenges in Kenya. *Marriage and Family Review*, 41(1–2), 47–70.

Njue, M. (2014, June 21). Personal Communication.

Njuguna, L. W. (2013). *Influence of Suburbanization on Real Estate Market Performance in Satellite Towns in Kenya: A Case of Kiambu Town* (Doctoral dissertation). University of Nairobi, Nairobi, Kenya.

Nnaemeka, O. (1994). From Orality to Writing: African Women Writers and the (Re)Inscription of Womanhood. *Research in African Literatures*, 25(4), 137–157.

Nyabuga, G. and Booker, N. (2013). Mapping Digital Media: Kenya. *Open Society Foundations*. Retrieved from http://www. opensocietyfoundations. org/sites/default/files/mapping–digitalmedia–kenya–20130321. pdf.

Nyagah, M (Producer/Director). (2013). *Uhiki: The Wedding: A Documentary on Culture and Environment*. Nairobi: Africa Health and Development International.

Nyamnjoh, F. B. (2011). De–Westernizing Media Theory to Make Room for African Experience. In H. Wasserman (Ed.), *Popular Media, Democracy and Development in Africa*, (pp. 19–31). London: Routledge.

Nzegwu, N. (1994). Gender Equality in a Dual–sex System: The Case of Onitsha. *The Canadian Journal of Law and Jurisprudence*, 7(1), 73–95.

Nzegwu, N. (1997). O Africa: Gender Imperialism in Academia. In O. Oyewumi (Ed.), *African Women and Feminism: Reflecting on the Politics of Sisterhood* (pp. 99–157). Trenton: Africa World Press.

Nzegwu, N. (2001). Globalization and the Jenda Journal. *Jenda: A Journal of Culture and African Women Studies*, 1(1), 1–17.

Nzegwu, N. (2002). Questions of Agency: Development, Donors, and Women of the South. *Jenda: A Journal of Culture and African Women Studies*, 2(1), 1–28.

Nzegwu, N. (2004a). Cultural Epistemologies of Motherhood. *JENdA: A Journal of Culture and African Women Studies*, 5, 1–4.

Nzegwu, N. (2004b). The Epistemological Challenge of Motherhood to Patriliny. *JENdA: A Journal of Culture and African Women Studies*, 0(5), n. p.

Nzegwu, N. (2005). Feminism and Africa: Impact and Limits of the Metaphysics of Gender. In K. Wiredu (Ed.), *A Companion to African Philosophy* (pp. 560–569). Malden: Blackwell Publishing Ltd.

References

Nzegwu, N. (2006). *Family Matters: Feminist Concepts in African Philosophy of Culture*. Albany: SUNY Press.
Nzegwu, N. (2009). Globalization and the Jenda Journal. *JENdA: A Journal of Culture and African Women Studies*, 1(1).
Oboler, R. S. (1980). Is the Female Husband a Man? Woman/Woman Marriage among the Nandi of Kenya. *Ethnology*, 19(1), 69–88.
Oboler, R. S. (1985). *Women, Power, and Economic Change: The Nandi of Kenya*. Palo Alto: Stanford University Press.
O'Brien, M. (1981). *The Politics of Reproduction*. Boston: Routlegde & Kegan Paul.
Ocholla–Ayayo, A. B. C. (1976). *Traditional Ideology and Ethics Among the Southern Luo*. Uppsala: The Scandinavian Institute of African Studies.
Odhiambo, T. (2007). Sexual Anxieties and Rampant Masculinities in Postcolonial Kenyan Literature. *Social Identities*, 13(5), 651–663.
Oduol, W. and Kabira, W.M. (1995). The Mother of Warriors and Her Daughters: The Women's Movement in Kenya. In A. Basu and C. E. McGrory (Eds.), *The Challenge of Local Feminisms: Women's Movements in Global Perspective* (pp. 187–208). Boulder, Colorado: Westview Press.
O'Keeffe, G. S. and Clarke–Pearson, K. (2011). The Impact of Social Media on Children, Adolescents, and Families. *Pediatrics*, 127(4), 800–804.
Olanga, C. A. (2015). *Impact of Firmographics, Expertise, Constraints and Constraint Management Methods on Weddings Organized by Wedding Planning Firms in Nairobi County, Kenya* (Doctoral dissertation). Kenyatta University, Nairobi, Kenya.
Olanga, C., Gesage, B. and Murungi, C. (2015). Planning Expertise, Variables Influencing Performance Outcomes and Management of Wedding Organization Firms in Nairobi County, Kenya. *African Journal of Tourism Hospitality and Leisure Studies*, 1(1), 1–28.
Olubayi, O. (2010). The Emerging National Culture of Kenya: Decolonizing Modernity. *Journal of Global Initiatives: Policy, Pedagogy, Perspective*, 2(2), 223–238.
Omwami, E. M. (2011). Relative-change Theory: Examining the Impact of Patriarchy, Paternalism, and Poverty on the Education of Women in Kenya. *Gender and Education*, 23(1), 15–28.
Ooms, T. and Wilson, P. (2004). The Challenges of Offering Relationship and Marriage Education to Low-income Populations. *Family Relations*, 53(5), 440–447.
Otieno, R. (2014). Family Law in Kenya: A Discussion: The State Has No Business Poking Its Nose into a Purely Private Institution Such As Marriage. *University of Nairobi School of Law* (Discussion paper), 1–16.
Otnes, C. C. and Pleck, E. (2003). *Cinderella Dreams: The Allure of the Lavish Wedding* (Vol. 2). Berkeley: University of California Press.
Otnes, C. and Scott L. M. (1996). Something Old, Something New: Exploring the Interaction between Ritual and Advertising. *Journal of Advertising*, 25(1), 33–50.
Owolabi, K. A. (2001). Globalization, Americanization and Western Imperialism. *Journal of Social Development in Africa*, 16(2), 71–92.
Oyewumi, O. (1997). *The Invention of Women: Making an African Sense of Western Gender Discourses*. Minneapolis: University of Minnesota Press.
Oyewumi, O. (2000). Family Bonds/Conceptual Binds: African Notes on Feminist Epistemologies. *Signs*, 25(4), 1093–1098.
Oyewumi, O. (2002). Conceptualizing Gender: The Eurocentric Foundations of Feminist Concepts and the Challenge of African Epistemologies. *Jenda: a Journal of Culture and African Woman Studies*, 2(1), 1–9.
Oyewumi, O. (2003). Abiyamo: Theorizing African Motherhood. *Jenda: A Journal of Culture and African Women Studies*, 4(1), 1–7.
Paechter, C. (2012). Bodies, Identities and Performances: Reconfiguring the Language of Gender and Schooling. *Gender and Education*, 24(2), 229–241.
Pala, A. (2010). The Ground We Stand On. Retrieved from http://www.womensmediacenter.com/feature/entry/the-ground-we-stand-on.

References

Pala, A. (2015). Dimensions of African Motherhood. *JENdA: A Journal of Culture and African Women Studies*, 0(23), 8–10.

Pala, A. O. (1977). Definitions of Women and Development: An African Perspective. *Signs*, 3(1), 9–13.

Parsitau, D. S. and Mwaura, P. N. (2010). God in the City: Pentecostalism as An Urban Phenomenon in Kenya. *Studia Historiae Ecclesiasticae*, 36(2), 95–112.

Pauli, J. (2013). Celebrating Distinctions: Common and Conspicuous Weddings in Rural Namibia. *Ethnology: An International Journal of Cultural and Social Anthropology*, 50(2), 153–167.

Pauli, J. (2010). The Female Side of Male Patronage: Gender Perspectives on Elite Formation Processes in Northwest Namibia. *Journal of Namibian Studies: History Politics Culture*, 8, 27–47.

Pauli, J. (2012). Creating Illegitimacy: Negotiating Relations and Reproduction within Christian Contexts in Northwest Namibia. *Journal of Religion in Africa*, 42(4), 408–432.

Pizzolato, J. E. (2006). Achieving College Student Possible Selves: Navigating the Space between Commitment and Achievement of Long–term Identity Goals. *Cultural Diversity and Ethnic Minority Psychology*, 12(1), 57–69.

Pollen, A. (2011). Performing Spectacular Girlhood: Mass–produced Dressing–up Costumes and the Commodification of Imagination. *Textile History*, 42(2), 162–180.

Pomerantz, S., Raby, R. and Stefanik, A. (2013). Girls Run the World? Caught Between Sexism and Postfeminism in School. *Gender and Society*, 27(2), 185–207.

Presley, C. A. (1992). *Kikuyu Women, the Mau Mau Rebellion and Social Change in Kenya*. Boulder: Westview Press.

Prince, R. J. (2013). Tarmacking' in the Millennium City: Spatial and Temporal Trajectories of Empowerment and Development in Kisumu, Kenya. *Africa*, 83(4), 582–605.

Quinn, A., Boneva, B., Kraut, R., Kiesler, S., Cummings, J., and Shklovski, I. (2003). Teenage Communication in the Instant Messaging Era. Retrieved from https://www.researchgate.net/profile/Sara_Kiesler2/publication/260297050_Teenage_communication_in_the_instant_messaging_era/links/553e44a80cf20184050df94e.pdf.

Rana, K. A. A. (1977). Class Formation and Social Conflict: A Case Study of Kenya. *Ufahamu: A Journal of African Studies*, 7(3), 17–72.

Rappaport, R. A. (2002). *The Ritual and Religion in the Making of Humanity*. Cambridge: Cambridge University Press.

Rarieya, J. F. A. (2007). *School Leadership in Kenya: the Lived Realities of Women Heads of Schools* (Doctoral dissertation). University of Keele, Keele, UK.

Ravallion, M. (2010). The Developing World's Bulging (but Vulnerable) Middle Class. *World Development*, 38(4), 445–454.

Reporter, D. M. (2011, July 22). Are Kate and Wills Planning a Family? Couple Save Top Tier of Wedding Cake for Christening of First Child. Retrieved from http://www.dailymail.co.uk/femail/article–2017554/Are–Kate–Middleton–Prince–William–planning–family–They–save–wedding–cake–tier.htm.l

Republic of Kenya Government Printer, The. (2014). The Marriage Act, 2014. *Kenya Gazette Supplement No. 62*, Acts no. 4, 31–69.

Resnick, D. (2015). The Political Economy of Africa's Emergent Middle Class: Retrospect and Prospects. *Journal of International Development*, 27(5), 573–587.

Ringrose, J. (2010). 12 Sluts, Whores, Fat Slags and Playboy Bunnies: Teen Girls' Negotiations of 'Sexy' on Social Networking Sites and at School. In C. Jackson, C. Paechter and E. Renold (Eds.), *Girls and Education, 3–16: Continuing Concerns, New Agendas* (pp.170–182). Berkshire: Open University Press.

Robinson, R., Hermans, C., Scheepers, P. and Schilderman, H. (2007). Your Big Wedding Day: Temporal Goal of Church Marriage Rituals. *Radboud University Nijmegen Repository*, 178–190.

References

Rodrigues, R. A. (2016). *Femvertising: Empowering Women through the Hashtag? A Comparative Analysis of Consumers' Reaction to Feminist Advertising on Twitter* (Doctoral dissertation). Instituto Superior de Economia e Gestão, Lisbon, Portugal.

Roney, C. and Editors of the Knot. (2014). *The Knot Little Books of Big Wedding Ideas: Cakes, Bouquets & Centerpieces, Vows & Toasts, and Details.* Potter Style.

Rutherford, J. (1990). The Third Space. Interview with Homi Bhabha. In: *Ders. (Hg): Identity: Community, Culture, Difference.* London: Lawrence and Wishart, 207–221.

Sanya, B. N. (2013). Disrupting Patriarchy: An Examination of the Role of E-technologies in Rural Kenya. *Feminist Africa, 18*, 12–24.

Sarvas, R. and Frohlich, D.M. (2011). *From Snapshots to Social Media: The Changing Picture of Domestic Photography.* London: Springer Science and Business Media.

Sawyer, S. M., Afifi, R. A., Bearinger, L. H., Blakemore, S. J., Dick, B., Ezeh, A. C. and Patton, G. C. (2012). Adolescence: A Foundation for Future Health. *The Lancet,* 379(9826), 1630–1640.

Schechner, R. (2013). *Performance Studies: An Introduction.* New York: Routledge.

Scott, E. S. (2002). The Legal Construction of Childhood. In M. K. Rosenheim (Ed.), *A Century of Juvenile Justice* (pp. 113–141). Chicago: University of Chicago Press.

Seekings, J. and Nattrass, N. (2002). Class, Distribution and Redistribution in Post–apartheid South Africa. *Transformation: Critical Perspectives on Southern Africa,* 50(1), 1–30.

Shaw, C. M. (1995). *Colonial Inscriptions: Race, Sex and Class in Kenya.* Minneapolis: University of Minnesota Press.

Shiino, W. (N.d.) A Mutually Complementary Relationship? The Condition of Single Women in Both Village and City in Kenya. Retrieved from http://www.tufs.ac.jp/ofias/j/caas/6_037–043%E3%80%80wakana%20shiino.pdf.

Simmons, A. (2002). Bedroom Politics: Ladies of the Night and Men of the Day. In Herbert, E. W., Knapp, A. B., Pigott, V. C. (Eds.), *Social Approaches to an Industrial Past: The Archaeology and Anthropology of Mining* (pp. 59–80). London/New York: Routledge.

Sklar, R. L. (1979). The Nature of Class Domination in Africa. *The Journal of Modern African Studies,* 17(04), 531–552.

Smith, D.J. (2010). Promiscuous Girls, Good Wives, and Cheating Husbands: Gender Inequality, Transitions to Marriage, and Infidelity in Southeastern Nigeria. *Anthropological Quarterly,* 83(1), 1–20.

Southall, R. (2004). Political Change and the Black Middle Class in Democratic South Africa. *Canadian Journal of African Studies,* 38(3), 521–542.

Spronk, R. (2009). Sex, Sexuality and Negotiating Africanness among Young Professionals in Nairobi. *Africa,* 79(4), 500–519.

Spronk, R. (2014). Exploring the Middle Classes in Nairobi: From Modes of Production to Modes of Sophistication. *African Studies Review,* 57(1), 93–114.

Steingraber, S. (2007). *The Falling Age of Puberty in US Girls: What We Know, What We Need To Know.* San Francisco: The Breast Cancer Fund.

Strano, M. M. (2006). Ritualized Transmission of Social Norms through Wedding Photography. *Communication Theory,* 16(1), 31–46.

Strode, M., Crawfurd, L., Dettling, S. and Schmieding, F. (2015). Jobs and the Labor Market. In M. Ncube and C.L. Lumpufa (Eds.), *The Emerging Middle Class in Africa,* (pp. 9–33). New York: Routledge.

Sudarkasa, N. (2004). Conceptions of Motherhood in Nuclear and Extended Families, with Special Reference To Comparative Studies Involving African Societies. *JENdA: A Journal Of Culture and African Women Studies,* 5, n.p.

Swai, E. V. (2006). (Re)Discovering Self Women's Construction of Identities: Socio–cultural View. *Adult Education Research Conference,* 385–390. Retrieved from http://newprairiepress.org/aerc/2006/papers/55.

Tamale, S. (2000). 'Point of Order, Mr Speaker': African Women Claiming their Space in Parliament. *Gender and Development,* 8(3), 8–15.

Therborn, G. (2004). Introduction: Globalization, Africa, and African Family Patterns. In T. Göran, (Ed.), *African Families in A Global Context, No. 131* (pp. 9–16). Uppsala: Nordic Africa Institute.

Thomas, L. M. (2003). *Politics of the Womb: Women, Reproduction, and the State in Kenya*. Berkeley and Los Angeles: University of California Press.

Thomas, S. S. (2000). Transforming The Gospel of Domesticity: Luhya Girls and the Friends Africa Mission, 1917–1926. *African Studies Review*, 43(2), 1–27.

Tomlinson, J. (2003). Globalization and Cultural Identity. In D. Held and A. McGrew (Eds.), *The Global Transformations Reader* (pp. 269–278). Cambridge: Polity Press.

Tschirley, D., Reardon, T., Dolislager, M. and Snyder, J. (2015). The Rise of A Middle Class in East and Southern Africa: Implications for Food System Transformation. *Journal of International Development*, 27(5), 628–646.

Vares, T., Jackson, S. and Gill, R. (2011). Preteen Girls Read 'Tween' Popular Culture: Diversity, Complexity and Contradiction. *International Journal of Media and Cultural Politics*, 7(2), 139–154.

Viere, G. M. (2001). Examining Family Rituals. *The Family Journal*, 9(3), 285–288.

Visagie, J. and Posel, D. (2013). A Reconsideration of What and Who is Middle Class in South Africa. *Development Southern Africa*, 30(2), 149–167.

Wagikondi, M. M. (2013). *An Investigation of Commuter Satisfaction in the Use of Muthurwa Terminus, Nairobi, Kenya* (Doctoral dissertation). University of Nairobi, Nairobi, Kenya.

Walker, L. (2000). Feminist in Bride Land. *Tulsa Studies in Women's Literature*, 19(2), 219–230.

Wambui, B. (2007). The Challenge of Provenance: Myth, Histories, and the Negotiation of Socio–political Space. *Praxis*, 19(2), 1–10.

Wambui, B. (2013). Conversations: Women, Children, Goats, Land (E. Mwangi, Trans.). In C. Jeffers (Ed.), *Listening to Ourselves : A Multilingual Anthology of African Philosophy* (pp. 91–123). Albany: SUNY Press.

Wane, N. N. (2000). Indigenous Knowledge: Lessons from the Elders–A Kenyan Case Study. In B. L. Hall, G. J. S. Dei and D. G. Rosenberg (Eds.), *Indigenous Knowledges in Global Contexts: Multiple Readings of Our World* (pp. 54–69). Toronto: University of Toronto Press.

Wedding Services Kenya. (n.d.). http://www.weddingserviceskenya.com.

Weinreich, P. (2009). 'Enculturation', not 'Acculturation': Conceptualizing and Assessing Identity Processes in Migrant Communities. *International Journal of Intercultural Relations*, 33(2), 124–139.

Wessell, A. (2012). Having Our Cake and Eating It Too: A Reading of Royal Wedding Cakes. *Australasian Journal of Popular Culture*, 2(1), 47–56.

Willett, R. (2008). Consumer Citizens Online: Structure, Agency, and Gender in Online Participation. In D. Buckingham (Ed.), *Youth, Identity, and Digital Media* (pp. 49–70). Cambridge, MA: The MIT Press.

Willis, J. L. (2009). Girls Reconstructing Gender: Agency, Hybridity and Transformations of 'Femininity'. *Girlhood Studies*, 2(2), 96–118.

Willy, A. M., Kimani, C. and Musiega, D. (2014). Investigation of the Operational Challenges Experienced by Hotels in Kakamega County. *The International Journal of Business and Management*, 2(5), 85–99.

Wilson, C. (2005). Wedding Cake: A Slice of History. *Gastronomica*, 5(2), 69–72.

Wiseman, R. (2009). Queen Bees & Wannabes: Helping your Daughter Survive Cliques, Gossip, Boyfriends, and the New Realities of Girl World. *Education Review*, 0, n.p.

Yankuzo, K. I. (2014). Impact of Globalization on the Traditional African Cultures. *International Letters of Social and Humanistic Sciences*, (15), 1–8.

Index

acculturation, xx
adolescence, 19, 23, 24; pre-, 24
adoption, 2, 4, 6, 15, 16n3
adulthood, 1, 5, 23, 26, 27, 28, 29, 36, 58, 64, 72
adulting, 28
Africanness, 40, 50
agency, x, xxiii; ELPs, 5, 7, 15, 30, 31, 37, 45, 58, 60, 72
agnatic kinship, 13
alloparents, xxii
altar, 48, 50, 51
Americanity, xii, 51
Americanization, xii, 20, 36
Americanness, 20
anatomy, 55; of a good wife, xxv
assisted reproductive technologies, 3

Babylon, ix, 20
banns, 45
bilineal, 14
bio-father, 12
bio-mother, 24; -hood, xxiv, 2, 4, 6
biologized patriliny, 13, 17n13
blood lines, 11, 13
bodies, x; bridal, xxiii, xxiv, 37; colonial organizing, xix; good and bad female, xix; wifing, xxiii, xxv, 55–68
boys in crisis, 75
breadwinners, 71
bridal: chorus, 50; expos, 41; shower, 40; shower gifts, 40
brideliness, xxiv, 39, 47, 52
bridezilla, 53n10
the British Parliament Legitimacy Ordinance, 14

capital centers, 74
capitalist machine, 76
celebration, 14, 31, 33, 40, 42, 47, 48, 67

cell group, 62
ceremony, 37, 51, 60; christening, xxiv; indigenous betrothal, 45; wedding, 37, 40, 41, 45, 48, 50
christening, xxiv
Christian womanhood, 3, 5, 7
churchwomanship, 56, 62
cityscapes, 76
cliquing culture, 31
codes, 31, 32, 33, 79; coming of age, 31; cultural, 80; maternal, 8; penal, 48; religious, 31; teenage, 32
colonial, xi; interruption, xix; Kenya, xix, 76; lens, xix; organizing of bodies, xix; roots of Kenya's contemporary middle class, xi
colonialism, xix, xx, 48, 55, 58, 69, 81
coming of age : codes, 31; institutions, xxiii; processes, 19, 28
conjugal : arrangement, 11; family, 11; partner, 3
constitution, 73, 76
consumer : media culture, 29; segments in Sub-Saharan Africa, xv
contract, 38, 48, 51, 56
contractual rituals, 38, 48
co-parenting, 6, 67
cosmopolitan professionals, xv
county governments, 73
courtship, 5
critical approaches, xxv
cultural : assimilation, xviii, xxi, 52; globalization, xxvi, 42; glocalization, xxi; transferences, xviii
culturally hybridized, xxii, 19
culture : change and mixing, xxi; flows, xiii, xx

degendering, 40, 65

deinstitutionalization, xxv, 59, 65
dependent independent, 29
de-urbanization, 78
devolution, 73, 74, 76, 78, 79
devolved government, 75
digital world, 32, 79
domestic space, 68, 69

economic : drivers, 74; power, 77
elective lone parenting, 1, 2, 5, 11
elitism, xiv, 20
empowered, 7, 77
engagement, 37, 44; ring, 43
exhibitionism, 42
expanding middle class, xiv, 73, 74, 75, 76
expenditure, xv, 70, 71
expressive practices, 79
Europeanization, 20, 36
Europeanness, 20
evangelicalism, xii

facebook, 21, 67, 79
familism, 64
family : culture, 6, 59, 61, 64, 65, 69; extended-, 5, 11, 14, 15, 21, 57, 59, 61, 62, 67; values, 56
father-free elective lone parenting, 8
fatherhood, 2, 8, 12, 14, 15, 17n13
father-stand-ins, 12
femininities, x, xxv, 57, 81
feminist, 30, 35, 57, 62, 67, 68; fathers, 67; post-, 29
femvertising, 77
first culture, xx
first kiss, 51, 59, 60

gender : equity, 75; justice, 75, 76; mainstreaming, 76
gendered : familial identities, 2; parenting, 22; parenting culture, 68
genital modifications, xxii
gentrifying, 74
gestational carriers, 2, 4
gift registries, 40
girl : cultures, 19, 20, 21, 22, 33; power, 77
globalization, xv, xxvi
good wifing, 55

gylanic, 6

heterosexual, xi, 6, 15, 38, 42
higher education, 75, 78
Hollywoodization, 20
household, 15, 29, 40, 56, 68, 71; head of, 15, 55, 71
housewifery, 55
hybridity, 48, 80, 81

identities, ix, x; classed, xxiii; maternal, xxii; social, xiii; wifing, xxv
infrastructure, xvi, 78
initiation, xxii, 26, 27, 30
institutionalized wifing, 63
intersubjectivity, 33
intra-cytal plasmic sperm injection, 4
in vitro fertilization, 2, 4, 12, 13

Kenyan : government, 73; constitution, 76
Kenyanness, 75
kinship, 8, 11, 13, 15, 59, 63
kiss, xxiii, 51, 59, 60, 67

ladies, xix
legal contract, 48
leisure, xv, 31, 41, 71, 74, 79
liberal, xxii
lifestyle, ix, xii, xv, 9, 20, 30, 52, 67, 69, 71, 74, 79
lineage, 8, 10, 11, 12, 13, 14, 15
lineal: duo-, 14; matri-, 13, 14, 15
lower middle class, xvii

male-centric, 8, 15
marginalization, xvi, xviii, 58, 75
marriage certificate, 38, 48, 49
marital roles, 65
masculinities, x, xxv, 57, 81
maternal codes, 8
maternity, 2, 5, 6
matriarchy, 1, 6, 8, 15
matricentric, 6
matrifocal, 6
matrilineal, 13, 14, 15
matrilineages, 15
matrilines, 1, 6
matrimonial : contract, 56; home, 40

Index

matristic, 6
maturity, 22, 23, 24, 28, 30
media, xx
middleclassness, xi, xiii, xiv, xix
missionary schools, 55
modern self-perceptions, xv
mother of the family, 6
mothering, xxii, 2, 6, 7, 9, 11, 13, 58, 66, 68
motherwork, xxii, 58, 65, 66
Mrs, 55, 56, 60, 63, 64
multilineal, 14
myth of independence, 19, 26

name change, 51, 63, 64
naming, 22, 24, 63; re-, 26, 57
nation state, xxvi, 48
neo-liberal, xxv
neopentecostal, xii, 62
neopentecostalism, xii
non-biological parenthood, 2
non-vulnerable middle class, xv
nuclear family, xxv, 3, 45, 55, 56, 59, 60, 61, 64, 65, 72
nuptial privacy, 61

other mothers, xxii

parental labor, 66
patriarchal : womanhood, 1, 8; wifehood, 58
patriarchy, xxii, 1, 6, 8, 12, 13, 15, 36, 43, 56, 62
patri-centered, x. *See also* male-centric, 8, 15
patrilineal, xi, 12, 13, 14, 15, 56
patriliny, xxii, 10, 12, 13, 15
peer-parents, 31
personhood, xxii, xxvi, 1
pinterest, 79
postfeminism, 29, 30
postnatal, 9
pre-adolescence, 24
preadolescent, 23
prenatal, 9
private schools, 74
private worlds, 58
privilege, 5, 16, 58
production, 20, 65, 66, 68, 71, 74, 75, 77

professional womanhood, 1
proposal, 37, 39, 44
puberty, 23, 24
public : world, 58; work force, 75

queer co-parenting, 6

radical wifing, 72
regional urban migration, 78
re-identification, 57
reproduction, 31, 50, 65
reproductive, 11; health, xxii; roles, 65, 66; wifehood, 66
rising strivers, xv
rite of passage, 27
ritual(s), xiii
rural elite, 79

satisfied middle class, xvii
self-centering, 64
self-concepts, 31
self-definition, x, xvii
self-identifying, xv
selfhood, 21, 28, 55, 57, 58, 60
self-(re)location, 59
self-representation, 21, 79
sexualization, 6, 11, 66
single mother, 1, 7, 11; - hood, 5, 7, 11
single professional woman, 1, 9
sisterhoods, 79
social fathers, 12
social : institutions, xviii, 22, 31; media, xxii, 20, 21, 29, 33, 41, 43, 77, 79, 80
socialization, 27, 31, 69; inter- and intra-, 79
spectacle, 42, 43
sperm, 3, 4, 10; bank, 10; donation, 10; donor, 11, 13; mate, 10
stigmatization, 5
struggling middle class, xvii
subcultures, ix, 79
sub-urbanization, 78
superbride, 42
surrogacy, 2, 12, 13
symbolic gifts, 40

technology driven world, 20
teen, 21, 23, 26, 27, 31; -age, xxii, 23, 31, 32; -ager, 26, 28, 29

thriving middle class, xvii
tourists, 80
trends, 73, 75, 77, 80
tv: commercials, 77; popular shows, 67; reality, 41
tween, 26, 27; -age, 23, 29; pre-, 27
twitter, 79

ubabi, ix
upper class, ix, xviii, xix, 74
upward mobility, xix, 78
urban centers, xvii, 73
urbanities, 74, 77
urbanization, 61, 76
usichana, 19

vanity resistance, 28, 30
veil, 51
vernacular FM radio stations, 80
virtual world, 32, 79
vows, 51
vulnerable adulthood, 58

wedding : aisle, 50; cake, xxiii, xxiv; committee, 45; dress, 46; pageant, 43; planner, 42, 43; ring, 51, 63
westernization, xi, xii, 9, 40
whatsapp, 21, 31
wifing bodies, 55, 58, 59, 61, 65, 68
wifization, 65
women cultures, ix
World Christian Database, xii

About the Author

Dr. Besi Brillian Muhonja is associate professor of Africana, and women's and gender studies in the Department of English at James Madison University. Her research, publication, and teaching areas of interest include critical African studies; critical gender and sexualities studies, decolonial and indigenous knowledges; Africana, transnational and subaltern feminisms; queer African studies; and motherhood studies. Her work has been extensively published in academic peer-reviewed journals and edited volumes. She is author of the book *Turn down the Volume on Silence*, and co-editor of the volume *Mothers and Sons: Centering Mother Knowledge*. She has served as editor for various peer-reviewed academic journals, and serves on a number of editorial and advisory boards.